HAS
Heaven
INVADED
Earth?

DAVID ADDESA

Burkhart Books

Bedford, Texas
www.burkhartbooks.com

Acknowledgments

In September of 2006 I read Bill Johnson's book, *When Heaven Invades Earth*. It would prove to be one of the most impacting books I have ever read. As an Assemblies of God pastor, I found Bill's journey similar to mine as it relates to actually trying to find and live out revival.

Over time, I have had the privilege of meeting some of the pastoral staff of Bethel church in Redding, California, and in particular Kris Vallotton. Though we have met on different occasions, I'm sure I'm simply a blur on Kris' horizon as he meets with thousands of people each year. Nevertheless, thank you Kris for your heart and your teaching on grace and judgment. Though I can't cite every idea that originates from your teaching, much of what is in this book has been birthed out of the revelation the Holy Spirit has given to you. I am greatly indebted to you.

In addition, the ministry of Graham Cooke, Dan McCollam, Danny Silk, Paul Manwaring have sprinkled my heart with understanding that is reflected in this work.

Personally, I'd like to thank Laura Sanford, Kelly Palmer, Tim Rush, and Jonathan Pettitt for their extraordinary help in the arduous task of editing this book. I'd also like to thank Victoria Moore, an up-and-coming leader in the Kingdom, for her striking cover art.

Finally, I'd like to thank my wife Lisa who is the unsung hero in our journey with Noah. Her inexorable dedication to the care and recovery of our son Noah has been his source of joy and hope. For me, it has catapulted my honor, love and respect for a woman I knew was fabulous when we married to even greater heights. No words can express how captivated I am with her beauty and character.

Lisa, you are a wellspring of life to the Addesa household.

Contents

Foreword

A message to the reader of this book, "Get yourself a box of Kleenex, a big drum ,and a strong, straight drum stick ,and prepare to stand up and swing the stick like your life depended on it!" Every once in a while hit that drum with that stick like you want it heard from Miami to New York and from San Diego to Seattle. Another thing, acquire the habit of moving toward the Kleenex box at warp speed, and grab, two (not one), dabbing each tear-filled eye. You're gonna weep, groan, snarl, shout, and hear yourself say such things as "Well, I never saw that before!" Or, "I can't believe what I am reading!" Even, "Wow, that is what I been trying to say and wanting to hear for years!" You will have difficulty putting this book down. You will find yourself returning to it after hours away from it, settling back into it like finding a new, old friend. Get ready to be revised.

David Addesa deserves to be heard and will be heard by a large segment of folks looking for reality. I reveled in his writing skills, weaving relevant Scriptures, great quotes, and powerful illustrations like a master tailor, weaving a costly garment. His faith has been forged in the furnace of affliction, beautifully and tastefully described at the beginning in "Noah's Story!"

David is a statesman, thus we can expect him to sound like one, and he does. At once taking the form of a powerful prophet pointing to inevitable warning signals of gathering judgment. At other times he stands an austere and timeworn Father speaking wisdom to his children. And still at other times, writing as a wise man setting forth powerful, and life-altering concepts for guidance to the deceived and the uninformed.

David is a warrior, whose family the devil has attempted to destroy. The warrior in him (and in them) fought back, and the devil winced in surprise at the raw strength and faith of this warrior and his family.

David is a worshiper, who at times so quantifies the eternal truths that we feel shame for our little faith, and find deep, inner determination to rise and journey on.

David is a thinker who leaves no deep mystery unaddressed and no precious doctrine unappreciated.

David is a judge with one thing on his mind—justice! A philosopher with one person on his heart— Jesus! A lover with one thing ever-pervading his mind—unconditional love for all, including the Trinity! In his writing is evidence of an amazing combination of gentleness and fierceness, of certainty and settledness without the slightest hint of arrogance.

Finally, David is a father who has found the Father's heart in the heavenlies, and puts all the Father's attributes into visible and audible sight and sound bites that whet our appetites for more and more.

"Atta boy, David!" I knew you could do it and I am pleased with you.

To you, dear reader, plunge into this work now, it's a great read!

Jack Taylor
President
Dimensions Ministries
Melbourne, Florida

Preface

THE EVENT THAT CHANGED EVERYTHING FOR ME

On April 27th, 2007 my eleven year old son Noah, was struck down by lightning. I was attending a conference in Mechanicsburg, Pennsylvania when I received a frantic call from my daughter. From that moment on life for the Addesa household was forever interrupted by an event that shook us to our core.

As I proceeded to call my personal assistant, she instructed me to go immediately to the airport because she had already changed my flight back home for that afternoon. Up to that point, all I knew was that Noah lay dead in our backyard for an unknown period of time, eventually being resuscitated by a local paramedic team.

As I sat in the Philadelphia airport, waiting for my flight home, it literally felt like the floor of my life disappeared from under me and I was being sucked into a malevolent vortex of hell. It was the darkest night of my soul. Upon arriving in the hospital, I walked into the ICU with my soul frozen in a wasteland of shock hoping for enough fortitude to help my family cope with this tragedy.

For the next few hours I felt like a dead man walking. As I walked down the hall of the third floor of ICU dozens of people from our church lined the halls and filled the waiting room. Emotionally moving as that could have been for me, I was incapable of acknowledging their presence. The best I could do was follow a friend who was leading me back to my wife and my son.

As I entered Noah's room another wave of dark despair rolled over me. Lying on his back, the first thing that caught my eye were the burns on Noah's chest and face where the bolt of lightning struck him. Anytime a million volts of electricity comes into contact with human flesh it immediately incinerates the once live tissue. Immediately, it became apparent that Noah's vitals were in complete dependency upon modern technology. As the electronic life support did it's duty Noah's body accepted each command. Every breath and heartbeat seemed almost synchronized like a fine tuned instrument.

In that moment I mustered every bit of strength I had just to keep myself from falling apart in front of my family. Through the years as pastor, I have visited ICUs with the hope of bringing encouragement and strength to families that had a loved one teetering in and out of consciousness. I used to privately speculate with my wife if people on full life support were actually "there" or was it simply machines caring out complex biological functions. When I walked into Noah's room my mind was flooded with those questions.

The medical team who cared for Noah were quick to point out that his curious movements were simply autonomic responses from his brain and not likely his will.

For the next three months, Noah was in a coma and had little response to outward stimuli initiated by the medical team or my family. From the outset of Noah's accident, the medical prognosis was bleak. Medical professionals advised Lisa and I to take Noah to a local care center for the severely disabled. It is a place without hope…a place where hopeless parents drop off their children to be cared for by professional caregivers for their remaining days. Within ten minutes of walking through the facility, we looked at each other and said, "What are we doing here?" We have Hope. His name is Jesus.

Weeks turned into months. In the early days of this journey, Noah began to wake up. His eyes were open but there was no emotional response from personal interactions. Despite the hopeless prognosis of the medical field, Noah began to progress in ways no one expected.

Four months after lightning left Noah dead in the mud in our back yard, the medical chief of staff said, "Noah is there … it's simply a struggle for him to synergize his intentions with coordinated muscle movements." *In layman's terms, Noah is no longer considered comatose.*

Three days after the medical chief pronounced that Noah was no longer comatose. Noah's doctor said his brain activity was normal. I pressed the doctor, wanting to know what he meant by *normal*. "Normal in the sense that his brain waves are that of a normal 11-year-old boy," the doctor explained. A little more than four months after Noah died and been revived, he returned home.

Looking back at my blog I made this observation: "Our opinion is that Noah clearly knows he is home, he knows his siblings, he knows his parents, and he knows his house. He even recognizes his dog." Things were beginning to turn.

During those early weeks with Noah, the why questioned became an echo in our hearts for days and weeks to come. *Why did this happen? Why did God allow this to happen? Why would a loving God do this to me and my family?* Once the *why* question remains unanswered, it gave way to the *what did I do…or not do to bring about this calamity in my son's life.* That singular event has set the tone for the rest of my life as it relates to God's activities on this planet.

The Church at large has been somewhat schizophrenic in her declaration of the love of God and His goodness to mankind. We have pointed out times of global trouble and regional catastrophes as the handiwork of a God who is judging us for our sinful behavior

As I am writing this introduction, our nation experienced the tragic slaughter of twenty grade school age children and six adults at an Elementary School in Newton Connecticut. A national evangelical leader was quick to point out that this horrid tragedy occurred in part by the judgment of God falling upon our nation in response to national sin. Though that may satisfy our sense of justice, the world outside the Kingdom reels with pain and grief. They would never follow a God who just killed their family members.

1 Kings 18 has always been one of my favorite chapters in the bible. In particular, it relates to our dark season with Noah's future in the balance…

Then Elijah said to Ahab, "Go up, eat and drink; for there is the sound of abundance of rain." So Ahab went up to eat and drink. And Elijah went up to the top of Carmel; <u>then</u>

he bowed down on the ground, and put his face between his knees, and said to his servant, "Go up now, look toward the sea." So he went up and looked, and said, "There is nothing." And seven times he said, "Go again." Then it came to pass the seventh time, that he said, "There is a cloud, as small as a man's hand, rising out of the sea!" So he said, "Go up, say to Ahab, 'Prepare your chariot, and go down before the rain stops you."

Now it happened in the meantime that the sky became black with clouds and wind, and there was a heavy rain. So Ahab rode away and went to Jezreel. Then the hand of the LORD came upon Elijah; and he girded up his loins and ran ahead of Ahab to the entrance of Jezreel.

It was a sky without clouds, a clear day and yet Elijah contends for the word of the Lord to come to pass. God promised Elijah that He would end the drought yet virtually nothing had changed.

Israel experienced three and a half years of cloudless skies (James 5:17-18). It was a very dry time. It was a time when any cloud would have been good.

It's easy to have what you see dictate how you pray and what you believe when you are looking at a cloudless, hopeless, sky. For this reason it is important that you be careful who you surround yourself with. I remember sitting with my wife in the office of the Noah's chief neurologist. We were faced with a cloudless sky as he declared to us that there was "no light at the end of the tunnel." As broken as I was I knew that I could not let that report stick to my soul. In retrospect, I also knew this experience would define my understanding of God's Providence and Sovereignty on the earth *today*.

Today, I believe you are about to discover aspects of God that I learned in my journey through the dark night of my soul. I stress *today* more than anything else because either God is judging the earth *today* or He is not. In other words, if God is good, why does He destroy people who rebel against Him? Does He in fact send catastrophes our way to correct our ways? There is no biblical gray area in these propositions. I believe this book will help you biblically sort out this paradox while not denying God's sovereignty. I invite you to lay aside presuppositions and allow Him to define His activities through His invaluable Word. The answers just might change the way you perceive Who He really is. I pray you will enjoy the journey. I have.

Introduction

When I shut up heaven and there is no rain, or command the locusts to devour the land, or send pestilence among My people if My people who are called by My name will humble themselves, and pray and seek My face, and turn from their wicked ways, then I will hear from heaven, and will forgive their sin and heal their land.

2 Chronicles 7:13-14 (KJV)

Over the years, this has become one of the most frequently used texts I know of in prayer movements around the world. It is referenced when calamity hits our shores or natural disasters overwhelm our people. One of my first recollections of the aftermath of 9/11 was the cry from some very prominent leaders in the American church that we had just encountered the consequence of the sin that prevails in our land. God was judging us.

In recent months I have begun to examine this powerful passage taken from the Old Testament in an attempt to sort out its application in our contemporary intercessory ministries across this great land. Let me make myself very clear. I am not "anointed" by God to undermine, dishonor or in any way rebuke the many existing prayer movements on the earth today. I'll leave that to someone else. My goal is to ask the questions and suggest ideas that may challenge how we view God's response to our cry for change. If the basis of our intercession is faulty, would not our expectation of God's response be likewise flawed?

Chapter 1 | JUDGMENT

THE DAYS OF ELIJAH

And it happened, while Apollos was at Corinth, that Paul, having passed through the upper regions, came to Ephesus. And finding some disciples he said to them, 'Did you receive the Holy Spirit when you believed?' So they said to him, 'We have not so much as heard whether there is a Holy Spirit.' And he said to them, '<u>Into what then were you baptized?</u>' So they said, 'Into John's baptism.' Then Paul said, 'John indeed baptized with a baptism of repentance, saying to the people that they should believe on Him who would come after him, that is, on Christ Jesus.' When they heard this, they were baptized in the name of the Lord Jesus.

Acts 19:1-5

It is significant to note here that Jesus said that John was "Elijah to come" (Matthew 17:12). The question Paul asked the disciples is a very important and one we probably still need to ask people in the church. I don't mean the baptismal formula that was used when you were baptized, but rather what is your understanding of <u>what</u> you were baptized into. There are many today who had a triune baptism (Father, Son and Holy Spirit), but still think and act like John the Baptist.

In my seminary days I used to tell my colleagues that there were two people in the New Testament I would not want to have as my pastor. One was Paul because he made his son Timothy be circumcised as an adult in order to become acceptable to the Jews. The other was John the Baptist because the guy was just plain scary. Turn or burn—that was his only sermon.

In Matthew 11:16-18, Jesus said that John came to sing the dirge and they did not morn, but He came playing the flute and they did not dance. In this metaphor Jesus was saying that the voice of prophecy in the Old Testament as climaxed in John's primary message is different than the voice of prophecy in the New Testament.

In Hebrews 1:1-2 it says:

God, who at various times and in various ways spoke in time past to the fathers by the prophets, has in these last days spoken to us by His Son...

In the tension of these two epoch seasons Jesus acknowledges that the religious leaders saw John in the wilderness eating locusts and honey and living a completely fasted lifestyle. He was the "Elijah to come." In contrast, Jesus came along and launched His miracle ministry at a wedding where all the guests were already pretty "happy" with wine. In response to His mother's request He created wine for celebrants to continue their festivity. In addition, He frequently associated with people who were living a "party" lifestyle. Most called them "sinners and tax collectors" or the "untouchables" of that day.

Can you see any contrast here even in their outward apparel? John had a camel hair cloak with a leather belt (like Elijah) and Jesus wore a seamless garment that was considered Prada or Gucci of His day. The soldiers gambled for it when He was crucified. The physical appearance of these two men underscored the cosmic shift in the making. Jesus summarized it this way in Luke 16:16, "*The law and the prophets were until John. Since that time the kingdom of God has been preached, and everyone is pressing into it.*" Something cosmic was beginning to shift.

CHANGE OF SEASONS

The most important thing you will ever have to address in your life is what is God really like to you. The key to this is to understand why Jesus came. He came to put a "face" on God.

He came to talk about favor, to present The Father in such a way that we could fully embrace and fully love. Isaiah 61 was Jesus' manifesto - His reason for being was to preach, open blind eyes, set captives free, etc. He came to play the flute so that we would no longer grieve and mourn, but would rejoice and dance. The gospel is about what God is really like.

This is how Jesus was known in Heaven before He ever came here. The Holy Spirit released that word to Isaiah so we could recognize Him when He arrived. Ultimately, He came to reveal the Father's heart to us.

In John 1:11, it says: *"He came to His own, and His own did not receive Him."* You see His people did not recognize Jesus because they had forgotten how God sees Himself. Generations before in Exodus 33:18 we see God provoking Moses to ask, *"God I want to see your glory."* So God put Moses in a place where he would be protected and when God passed by him it was like there was a divine parade, and at the head of the parade was God Himself marching past Moses.

God described Himself this way in Exodus 34:6-7:

> *Yahweh! The LORD! The God of compassion and mercy! I am slow to anger and filled with unfailing love and faithfulness I lavish unfailing love to a thousand generations. I forgive iniquity, rebellion and sin. But I do not excuse the guilty. I lay the sins of the parents upon their children and grandchildren. The entire family is affected—even children in the third and fourth generations. (NLT)*

As best as I can tell this is the first time God really talks about Himself in this manner. It is who He is. It is how He is known in Heaven. This statement is both profound and prophetic. It is profound because it describes a God who most people thought was only to be feared and not to be loved. I mean how can you love a bolt of lightning, or a burning bush, or a trembling mountain? It was prophetic because it would become the core of Jesus' ministry message.

What would it look like if you took two of the grand prophetic prototypes of the Old Testament, Elijah and Elisha, and had them come through the cross? On this side of "that" cross (Old Testament) they caused famines and drought. One killed 450 prophets of Baal, prophesied against kings and another cursed 42 children who called him baldy by having two bears tear them up. In addition, with lightning Elisha toasted two regiments of fifty men that came out to bring him to King Ahaziah, (2 Kings 1:9-14; 2:24).

What would happen if you took these scary men and had them transition their ministry through the other side of the cross (New Testament).

Malachi 4:5-6 says:

In the last days I will send Elijah the prophet...(Oh boy... not him ☺). He will turn the hearts of the father's to the children and the hearts of the children toward the fathers.

What happened?

When he moved from the Old Testament to the New Testament his ministry profile changed. God didn't change, the prophet's ministry profile changed. The entirety of the Old Testament was that the "wages of sin is death." It specified the ugliness and wretchedness of sin and mankind's hopelessness in entering into God's Kingdom. Paul refers to it as a ministry of death because when it came alive he died.

Over the years I have heard people say they have a hard time believing God would require the slaughter of so many animals. It seems as if God delighted in every drop of shed blood. That was not the case; rather it was to remind us that we need a Savior and sin is horrid. No one could keep the whole law. It said God is just, and because this is so, He must execute justice on the guilty.

So back in Exodus 34: 6-7 when God described Himself He said:

The God of compassion and mercy! I am slow to anger and

filled with unfailing love and faithfulness. I lavish unfailing love to a thousand generations. I forgive iniquity, rebellion, and sin. <u>But I do not excuse the guilty.</u> I lay the sins of the parents upon their children and grandchildren. The entire family is affected, even children in the third and fourth generations.

<u>*"But I do not excuse the guilty."*</u> God created justice through the cross so that He could remain a God of justice. And through the cross He now releases mercy and grace. **It is the good news of the Kingdom.**

Your understanding of God cannot depend upon your performance. Why? Because your performance is subject to change and He is unchanging. Your approach to God does not change His approach to you. Didn't Jesus tell us that He sends rain on the just and the unjust? In this context rain is understood to mean "blessing."

Matthew 5:43-48 says:

You have heard that it was said, You shall love your neighbor and hate your enemy. But I say to you, Love your enemies, bless those who curse you, do good to those who hate you, and pray for those who spitefully use you and persecute you that you may be sons of your Father in heaven; for He makes His sun rise on the evil and on the good, and sends rain on the just and on the unjust. For if you love those who love you, what reward have you? Do not even the tax collectors do the same? And if you greet your brethren only, what do you do more than others? Do not even the tax collectors do so? Therefore you shall be perfect, just as your Father in heaven is perfect.

Any prophetic word you hear must reflect these attributes of God. The voice of prophecy that makes you feel like "the beloved," that would be Him. The voice of God affirms you, even though you are in the process of changing. Please note that this would not be the enemy speaking. He would rather pluck his tongue out than tell you how much God loves you, or shows mercy and kindness.

Even in the midst of His rebuke or correction, I still feel wonderful about myself. God helps me to clean up my mess and never condemns me through that process. He doesn't provoke guilt or shame, and when it's complete I feel like saying, "Thank you Father for correcting me." He will tell you the truth in such a way that it will set you free to actually become that truth.

The voice of the Lord is kind, loving, uplifting, and can sometimes have some humor to it. But don't take my word for it, study it yourself. Because He is that to you; He will be that to you all the days of your life. The prophetic is really about hearing from the heart of God. Why is this important? Because the way you hear from God, and the way you connect with God, will ultimately become the way you connect with people.

I cannot count the many times over the years when I have been at the gym, or marketplace setting with friends I have made there. In particular, men, who find out I'm a pastor and say things like, "Man…why didn't you tell me you were a pastor? I wouldn't have talked like that." It is in those moments that I can be a minister of reconciliation.

2 Corinthians 5:18-19 says:

And all of this is a gift from God, who brought us back to himself through Christ. And God has given us this task of reconciling people to him. For God was in Christ, reconciling the world to himself, no longer counting people's sins against them. And he gave us this wonderful ministry of reconciliation. (NLT)

Also, Colossians 1:19-20 says:

For it pleased the Father that in Him all the fullness should dwell, and by Him to reconcile all things to Himself, by Him, whether things on earth or things in heaven, having made peace through the blood of His cross.

Do I need a degree from a Bible college or seminary to be a minister of reconciliation? Nope. You are a child of the King. Paul said that in Jesus God was reconciling the world to Himself. How? He did not count their sins against them. And when we walk in that ministry we become ambassadors who, if necessary, beg people to be reconciled to God.

For many people it's the first time in their lives they have heard the prophetic voice of God.

John said it better than I in John 3:16-17:

For God so loved the world that He gave His only begotten Son that whosoever believes in Him will have everlasting life." And here's the capstone next verse, "For God did not send His Son into the world to judge it, but by Him that it might be saved.

And so the question I would like to ask is this, "Was Jesus judged enough for all sin? If your answer is "No" then your very place in the Kingdom may be in question. You may have the mindset that Jesus was judged enough for your sin, but not for the sin of the most despicable criminal out there. Most of us have had people we know personally or through media that we find reprehensible. It could be your ex-spouse or a drunk driver who killed your loved one.

So when Paul said that in Christ God was reconciling the world to Himself by not counting their sins against them (2 Corinthians 5:19), he was saying that everything and everyone is now reconciled to Him. And those of us who have personally accepted this now become "the redeemed." So within a reconciled world the church becomes the redeemed community. This side of the cross (New Testament) the whole world is reconciled to

Him. And when you come through the cross, you now become the redeemed.

To not accept redemption is like getting your new credit card in the mail, but you cannot access the benefits of that card until first you connect with the source. The world is reconciled to God but cannot have access to the benefits until it first connects with the source, Jesus Christ. Are you getting this?

And so if this is true - and it is - there remains no more judgment from God until the day of judgment at His second coming.

That day is referred to in 2 Timothy 4:1:

I charge you therefore before God and the Lord Jesus Christ, who will judge the living and the dead at His appearing and His kingdom.

In order for God to judge anyone, as many say he does, it would be like ignoring the very blood of the sacrifice His Son gave. The church gets schizophrenic on this one. We speak and we act as though God only judged 95 percent of the sin and reserved five percent for places like San Francisco, Hollywood or wherever. The truth is that 100 percent of mankind's sin has already been judged on the cross.

However, when you have prophets prophesying judgment on "wherever", they are not false prophets in the biblical sense. They are prophets who release bad prophecies because of their poor understanding of God in the New Testament. If Jesus is only 95 percent judged, then none of us can know if we are saved ☺. I mean who's to say that I'm not in the five percent, "sad sack, sorry you're going to hell crowd." If He poured out every ounce of judgment and wrath upon Jesus, which He did, He doesn't have any left.

Between that cross, and the end of the age, there is no judgment until the last "day" and the Great White Throne judgment.

Revelation 20:11-15 says:

Then I saw a great white throne and Him who sat on it, from whose face the earth and the heaven fled away. And there was found no place for them. And I saw the dead, small and great, standing before God, and books were opened. And another book was opened, which is the Book of Life. And the dead were judged according to their works, by the things which were written in the book. The sea gave up the dead who were in it, and Death and Hades delivered up the dead who were in them. And they were judged, each one according to his works. Then Death and Hades were cast into the lake of fire. This is the second death. And anyone not found written in the Book of Life was cast into the lake of fire.

The bottom line is that judgment for the unbeliever is absolutely not until the end of the age.

Therefore the issue is about those who are reconciled and those who are redeemed.

1 John 2:1 says,

"My little children, these things I write to you, so that you may not sin. And if anyone sins, we have an advocate with the Father, Jesus Christ the righteous."

Do we believe that? The term advocate is derived from the law courts and means the counsel for the defense who stands alongside the accused. This concept finds its roots in Judeo-Christian theology. If Jesus is our advocate, our lawyer in the courts of Heaven, then surely the prophetic cannot become the prosecution against those whom Jesus reconciled to Himself. In a manner of speaking, you do not want to enter into a courtroom with Him as the defender of the sinner whom He has reconciled (but who are not yet redeemed).

One of the clearest statements Jesus ever said to us is found in Luke 6:37-38:

> *Judge not, and you shall not be judged. Condemn not, and you shall not be condemned. Forgive, and you will be forgiven. Give, and it will be given to you: good measure, pressed down, shaken together, and running over will be put into your bosom. For with the same measure that you use, it will be measured back to you.*

So the prophetic is not about judgment, it is about freedom. It points to who people are and what they can become. They are reconciled to God and if they come to Him on those terms and invite Jesus into their lives they now join the ranks of the redeemed. It is about speaking life where there once was death. It is about calling that which is not, as though it were. In the world we are supposed to be like the person in Sam's club who holds out a new food product to get us to taste it. To say, "Taste and see that the Lord is good." When the voice of prophecy comes into alignment with that, it supports the gospel of the Kingdom and does not oppose it. Poor prophecy is when it doesn't do that.

Poor prophecy is when you side step what Jesus said and begin to align with the wrong spirit which, by the way, sells a lot of books and generates revenue for those promoting the judgments of cities and nations. The prophetic must flow in the same river as the gospel does. Poor prophecy makes people feel condemned, ashamed and full of fear.

There is a difference between what is truth and what is true. It may be true that a person is a liar or a thief or full of anger. But the truth is that they don't have to remain that way. They can become a new creation in Christ. It is true that cities like San Francisco are known for their gross sin, but the truth is that it doesn't have to be like that. And when you are speaking the truth in love you can say, "Hey…you don't have to do that because this is who God says you are." The prophetic follows the way of truth.

It follows the person of Jesus.

You and I can then come along and be empowered by the prophetic voice to announce that all of the world is reconciled to Him. Now the unsaved no longer have to act in the habitual manner they once did. They can be redeemed by Him and will no longer be slaves to sin. It allows them to upgrade from reconciliation to redeemed.

Prophecy connects people with the source, so that they can see themselves not as they are, but as they could be. Any word that doesn't give you an upgraded understanding of who you are in Christ is poor prophecy.

DOES GOD JUDGE NOW?

I have found it notable to simply allow scripture to answer this question apart from the prognostications of men. Though this book asserts mine, and other assertions in this regard, it is good for us to allow the words of Jesus to set the parameters for this important question.

John 3:16-17 says:

For God so loved the world that He gave His only begotten Son, that whoever believes in Him should not perish but have everlasting life. 17 For God did not send His Son into the world to condemn the world, but that the world through Him might be saved.

John 5:22:

For the Father judges no one, but has committed all judgment to the Son...

John 5:26-27:

For as the Father has life in Himself, so He has granted the

David Addesa

Son to have life in Himself, and has given Him authority to execute judgment also, because He is the Son of Man.

John 9:39:

And Jesus said, "For judgment I have come into this world, that those who do not see may see, and that those who see may be made blind.

John 12:47-48 says:

And if anyone hears My words and does not believe, I do not judge him; for I did not come to judge the world but to save the world. He who rejects Me, and does not receive My words, has that which judges him—the word that I have spoken will judge him in the last day."

CHAPTER 2 | JOURNEY THROUGH GRACELAND[2]

And the Word became flesh and dwelt among us, and we beheld His glory, the glory as of the only begotten of the Father, full of grace and truth. John bore witness of Him and cried out, saying, 'This was He of whom I said, He who comes after me is preferred before me, for He was before me.' And of His fullness we have all received, and grace for grace. For the law was given through Moses, but grace and truth came through Jesus Christ.

John 1:14-17

In the New Testament the word grace "charis" is used 148 times. However, when we have it translated by reputable scholars they have a variety of words in English that mean grace. It's the classic one diamond with many facets metaphor. Other than grace it can be translated: favor, credit, thanks and gifts, besides the many times it is used as a greeting or blessing.

The word grace in the Old Testament is used less than half as many times as in the New Testament and most often means favor with God or man.

In the "Law and the Prophets" it is used only 24 times. Why am I giving you these statistics? So that you can see that verse 17 of John 1 really means what it says. Could it be that Jesus came to bring a culture of grace to the people of God that they had never known before?

Jesus came as an Apostle of grace. He didn't come to conquer, but conquer He did. He brought with Him the culture of the Kingdom which is held together by grace. This culture of grace has core values. One is called honor. Jesus said in Mark 6:4 that *"A prophet is not without honor except in his own country and among his own relatives (house). Now He could do no mighty work there(Nazareth), except that He laid His hands on a few sick people and healed them*". Honor is the gateway to Kingdom reward and Kingdom inheritance. The people of Jesus' home town lost both reward and inheritance in their flagrant dishonor of the One who came to heal them.

Another value is covenant. The covenant of Abraham and Moses both required faith and the shedding of blood. Covenants were legal transactions between two parties to ratify the conditions of a solemn agreement. One of the more common types of covenants was the purchase of land or houses. The only way out of the covenant was the death of one party. In other words, in order to change the terms of the agreement someone had to die.

So God gives the law to Moses and it is based upon a blood covenant. God then says He is going to change the covenant, so who has to die? He does. Let's pretend for a moment that Jason and his wife Cindy are friends of mine. Let's also pretend that Jason committed a crime that deserved capital punishment which required his life. Though his wife Cindy never denied her husband's crime, she went before the presiding judge and offered her life for his because the law demanded that a life be given for the life taken. The law required that someone die.

Well if you take that same scenario with the Judge of the Universe and apply that same appeal there is a problem. You see, God's law says that the wages of sin is death. So if Cindy went before that Judge and said, "Take my life for his." He would check the record and say, "Wait a second, we have a warrant out for your arrest as well. Sorry, you can't pay for him because you owe your life for yourself." Cindy is as guilty as her husband in the sight of God's law, because Cindy is guilty of sin.

Justice must be served. Jesus, because He had no sin, satisfied the justice the law required where no one else could. Jesus created justice within the cross. When He did that He could then dispense mercy. Why did God not extend mercy in the Mosaic Covenant? Because He would be like a judge on the take; a corrupt judge who makes deals when He feels like it. So the people of God lived in a culture of justice under Moses. The prophets prophesied out of it, the priests minister in it, and the people were surrounded by it.

That's why when Jesus was confronted with the woman caught in adultery (John 8) the Pharisees were not wrong in challenging Jesus about stoning her. The law demanded it. And though He was about to transition His people from law to grace He does something amazing. He doesn't say don't stone her. Instead He begins to introduce grace on the scene. He says something like, "Go ahead and stone her, but let's do it this way." Form the line over here, and whoever is without sin gets to throw the first stone. Deuteronomy 17:7 says that the one who witnessed it would be the first to cast the stone. Jesus comes along, bends down and begins to write in the dirt.

Jeremiah 17:13 says:

They that depart from me shall be written in the earth.

My personal conviction is that Jesus was writing the sins of the accusers on the ground in full view of those ready to stone the woman. Jesus was not excusing this woman's sin. He was simply pointing out that the whole lot of them were guilty so why stop with her?

And an amazing thing happened. One by one they dropped their stones and walked away. Eventually she looked at Jesus and He asked her if there was anyone left to stone her. She said, "No." At that moment she was looking into the eyes of the only one on the planet who could offer her mercy!

Let me ask you something? What are we offering people? A ten step program? A required list of things they must achieve before they are released from their guilt and shame. No, we are offering them life, not the old life, but a new life. I have often heard "I'm just a sinner saved by grace." What? Wait a minute... who told you that? The Bible says you are a new creation.

2 Corinthians 5:17 says:

*Therefore, if anyone is in Christ, he is a new creation; old
things have passed away; behold, all things have become
new.*

Search the New Testament. Paul never says to the sinners
saved by grace, peace to you. Instead He says *the Kingdom is
not a Kingdom of sinners but a Kingdom of saints!* (Romans 1:7;
15:25-26; 1 Corinthians 1: 2; 6:1) If we don't believe that a prosti-
tute can become a woman of grace, or a drug addict can become
a productive person, or a terrorist can find Jesus and become a
lover and not a hater, what in the world do we believe? After all,
some of you reading this book would be ostracized by many in
the church if they really knew your former lifestyle.

I remember 9/11 like it happened yesterday. I remember
there was a swirl of prophetic people who were basically saying
that God was serving us our just desserts for our sins. He was
judging us. In a manner of speaking, they were saying the event
was our fault because of all of the things we do wrong in this
land. It amounts to saying that the cross did not cover our sins of
the past, not to mention present and future. Really?

Do you think that any of the thousands who died on that
day in New York, Washington and Pennsylvania were believers?
Jesus said you and I are supposed to be salt and light. What does
that mean? Does that mean that if you come back to church for
tonight's service you should be so lit up for Jesus that we don't
need to turn on the sanctuary lights? No. It means that you and
I are revelators. Your life you can become a living illustration of
the Gospel of the Kingdom. When people see you, they see some
facet of Jesus.

What is salt? It's preservation. In biblical times they didn't
have vacuum packed freezer options. Salt was it. They would
catch their fish, salt them down, and then eat them at another time. Salt was a valuable commodity. If you were poor you
re-used the salt. How would you know if the salt was no longer

good? You'd taste it ☺. If it tasted less like salt and more like the fish head soup it was supposed to infuse, you'd throw it out ☺. It would be used for roads. You and I are revelation and preservation.

Therefore if we are supposed to be salt and light, and yet we prophesy destruction upon a sinful world, have we lost our savor? And if God caused 9/11 to happen to us, and Christians died in that tragedy, something is wrong with that picture. Are you seeing this?

My wife Lisa and I have a last will and testament. It does not go into effect until we die. The benefits of that testament are of no use to my family until we are gone. So when Jesus died He did so to leave a testament. And what He left you was a Kingdom. He said *"It's the Father's good pleasure to give you The Kingdom"* (Luke 12:32). That Kingdom is inhabited by saints, not sinners. Listen to Paul's salutation to the churches he was leading:

Romans 1:7:

To all who are in Rome, beloved of God, called to be saints...

1 Corinthians 1:2:

To the church of God which is at Corinth, to those who are sanctified in Christ Jesus, called to be saints...

2 Corinthians 1:1:

To the church of God which is at Corinth, with all the saints who are in all Achaia...

Ephesians 1:1:

To the saints who are in Ephesus, and faithful in Christ Jesus.

Philippians 1:1:

To all the saints in Christ Jesus who are in Philippi, with the bishops and deacons…

Colossians 1:2:

To the saints and faithful brethren in Christ who are in Colosse.

Why do you think Paul kept reminding them who they were over and over again? If you keep identifying people by who they used to be, you keep alive the law that condemned them, not the blood that cleansed them. I am thankful for support groups like Alcoholics Anonymous and others like them, but if I was an alcoholic and God delivered me from that bondage, I shouldn't keep identifying myself as an alcoholic. Grace has given me a new identity. Do you think if Jesus ran into the same women He forgave as adulterer that He would say, "Oh look…there's that adulterer?" No! Grace would say, "Look there is an amazing woman of grace…a daughter of the King…a saint who is living in Graceland because the Kingdom is a culture of grace.

MORE TIME IN GRACELAND

Those of my generation might think I am talking about Elvis' Graceland mansion in Tennessee that will cost you about $70 per person to enter. Its worldwide notoriety comes from one of the first "American Idols," none other than Elvis Presley. It was the place of his residence and has become a thriving tourist attraction for decades. Some have postulated that Elvis became more popular in death than in life because of this property.

Be that as it may, I'm borrowing this word "Graceland" to describe something more popular and more profound than any human existence could provide. That "Graceland" is not a memorial to a bygone musical star, but a description of the length and width and breadth of the culture of The Kingdom of God on the earth today. The Graceland I am talking about is so expensive that even wealthy people cannot afford the ticket.

John 1:14-17 says:

And the Word became flesh and dwelt among us, and we beheld His glory, the glory as of the only begotten of the Father, full of grace and truth. John bore witness of Him and cried out, saying, 'This was He of whom I said, He who comes after me is preferred before me, for He was before me. And of His fullness we have all received, and grace for grace. For the law was given through Moses, but grace and truth came through Jesus Christ.

For the sake of illustration, I am equating Graceland with the New Testament. When I say New Testament, most people think of books starting with Matthew and ending with Revelation in the Bible. The book of Hebrews says that Jesus is the Apostle and High Priest of our faith. The word Apostle was a word Jesus borrowed from the Romans. It described a group of special generals in the Roman army who did not just conquer people, but brought with them the culture of Rome. Have you ever heard of "The Apostles Creed?" It was formulated by the early church in an effort to consolidate the essentials of Christianity into one statement of faith. So that whether it was in India or Spain or Africa the apostolic belief system would remain consistent with the Chief Apostle Jesus Christ.

The people who were conquered by Rome did not lose their ethnic distinctiveness, but were taught the values and culture of Rome. They ultimately would look to Rome as their source of prosperity, safety and blessing. Hopefully, their loyalty to Rome would not be because they saw Roman soldiers patrolling their city streets, but because they truly enjoyed a life they did not have before Roman culture was introduced in their land.

THE BEGINNING OF THE JOURNEY

There is a scene in the New Testament often referred to as the "Road to Emmaus." It could be compared with the new journey into Graceland that Israel was about to discover. It occurred the day Jesus rose from the dead. In this scene, Jesus is walking with His disciples, yet they did not know it was Him.

Luke 24:19-21 says:

The things that happened to Jesus, the man from Naza-reth," they said. "He was a prophet who did powerful miracles, and he was a mighty teacher in the eyes of God and all the people. But our leading priests and other religious leaders handed him over to be condemned to death, and they crucified him. We had hoped he was the Messiah who had come to rescue Israel. (NLT)

Acts 1:6-8 adds:

Therefore, when they had come together, they asked Him, saying, 'Lord, will You at this time restore the kingdom to Israel?' And He said to them, 'It is not for you to know times or seasons which the Father has put in His own authority. But you shall receive power when the Holy Spirit has come upon you; and you shall be witnesses to Me in Jerusalem, and in all Judea and Samaria, and to the end of the earth.

There is an interesting consistency happening here. In the Luke passage the disciples were hoping for a literal restoration of the nation of Israel to its former glory. Again in Acts 1 the disciples were essentially asking the same question. Between Luke 24 and Acts 1 there were about 40 days and the disciples had the same basic misunderstanding regarding the purpose behind Jesus' mission. Notice the last phrase in Acts 1, "…and to the end of the earth." It took about ten years for them to get that message.

During that period, Peter and the rest of the disciples only took The Gospel of The Kingdom to other Jews. God finally sent an angel to a Gentile Roman soldier and told him to fetch Peter so he could hear the gospel. Peter then has a vision from God that corrects his incomplete doctrine of salvation (Acts 10). And now the church is back on track with God's original plan. Jews first and then Gentiles, and eventually back to Jews again (Romans 11).

But there was still some confusion in the church. Imagine that I am standing on a platform in front of you and on my right is a table with the Ten Commandments displayed in stone tablets. Then on my left is the cross that Jesus died upon. If I were to ask you, "Which of these symbols represents the Gospel of the Kingdom?" In the early church many were saying both.

So, the Church held a council in Jerusalem somewhere between 48 to 52 AD and decided that it is the cross and the cross alone. In fact Peter put it this way in Acts 15: 11 "But we believe that through the grace of the Lord Jesus Christ we shall be saved in the same manner as they."

Why the 20 year struggle to comprehend grace and grace alone? For those living under the law, it is really a challenge to live under grace. Their identity as a Jew was very much undermined with the setting aside of the old covenant. The Gentiles however had little understanding of the Law of Moses and the extreme weight of compliance required under that system.

In Luke 4, Jesus announces His ministry by quoting Isaiah 61.

Luke 4:18-19 says:

The Spirit of the Lord is upon Me, because He has anointed Me to preach the gospel to the poor; He has sent Me to heal the brokenhearted, to proclaim liberty to the captives and recovery of sight to the blind, to set at liberty those who are oppressed; To proclaim the acceptable year of the Lord.

There is a phrase missing here that is actually in the Old Testament version of Isaiah 61:2, "...*and the day of vengeance of our God.*" Now maybe this doesn't fascinate you like it does me, but Jesus is literally reading from the scroll of Isaiah. He skips over that verse intentionally. Let me tell you why I think he did that. John 3:16 says, "*God gave His only begotten Son that whosoever believes in Him should not perish but have everlasting life*". Verse 17 then says, "*For God sent not the Son into the world to judge the world; but that the world should be saved through him.*"

Now to John 5:22, "For the Father judges no one, but has committed all judgment to the Son." Furthermore, Jesus said that He did not come to judge. So since all of this judgment that the world deserves has been held at bay by grace, we therefore are in the age of grace. But there is a <u>day</u> coming when Jesus will return and judge His enemies. Until then we have a message of grace to release all over the planet.

So the Father judges no one...He's given that to His Son. Jesus tells us He doesn't judge either, but there is coming a day of judgment. Until that day comes, He judges no one. The question begs to be asked: "Then why do we judge?"

THE DAY OF JUDGMENT

2 Peter 3:7 says:

> *But the heavens and the earth which are now preserved by the same word, are reserved for fire until the day of judgment and perdition of ungodly men.*

Grace causes us to be a preserving agent on this planet. But there is a reservation as well. There is a "day" when this time of grace is over. And when it is over, the refining fire of judgment will purge the earth of ungodly angels and ungodly men. Paul gets very personal on this matter of judging.

1 Corinthians 4:3-5 says:

I care very little if I am judged by you or by any human court; indeed, I do not even judge myself. My conscience is clear, but that does not make me innocent. It is the Lord who judges me. Therefore judge nothing before the appointed time; wait till the Lord comes. He will bring to light what is hidden in darkness and will expose the motives of men's hearts. At that time each will receive his praise from God. (NIV)

So Paul is saying that judgment is reserved for a "<u>day</u>." In fact even as he was dictating this letter he could not find anything in himself that was wrong or worthy of judgment. But that did not acquit him. He said that a day is coming when there is full disclosure. God will allow us to see our own hearts, not to condemn us, but to correct us and commend us. Did you get that? In simple terms don't judge other people because you don't even know what might be worthy of judgment in you.

Let me give you an example of this spirit of judgment. I thought I would choose my denomination as an example. I searched the Assemblies of God on the Internet and within 30 seconds found this website from a so-called Christian apologist. Here is an excerpt from the website:

There are several Biblical heresies which are prevalent in the Assemblies of God churches. For example: they teach that you can lose your salvation. They also practice the unbiblical confusion of speaking in tongues. In addition, the Assemblies of God are known for their hands-on faith-healing services. One of the biggest wolves in the Assembly of God camp is (*name removed by author*). Other wolves within the Assemblies of God are: (*author has chosen to delete these names*). This is the tip of the iceberg of many scoundrels in the Assembly of God denomination who use the sheep for their own gain. Elvis Presley was also a member of the Assemblies of God. (*name removed by author*), one of the most hideous false prophets of our time, is also a member of the Assemblies of God.[3]

I do not agree with these statements and I have removed the names of the accused to end the cycle of judgment. I left the name of Elvis to demonstrate the ridiculous levels to which some will stoop. I included this quote to help you discern between disagreement in love concerning doctrine and judging someone. When you resort to phrases like, "biggest wolves, other wolves, scoundrels, and hideous false prophets," you have become a severe judge of the body, and you have no biblical justification to do so.

So Jesus said the Father has given all judgment over to Him. Then Jesus said He did not come to judge the world but to offer salvation. Paul and Peter agree that there is coming a day when judgment comes. So is there any judgment left for us to administrate? I hope you said no. Let me say, it is reserved for the church to discipline immorality and illegal or illicit conduct of its leaders and members. However, that is very clearly covered in the New Testament.

MERCY

Let's talk about another core value in Graceland. James 2:8-13 says:

Yes indeed, it is good when you obey the royal law (emphasis added) as found in the Scriptures, 'Love your neighbor as yourself.' But if you favor some people over others, you are committing a sin. You are guilty of breaking the law. For the person who keeps all of the laws except one is as guilty as a person who has broken all of God's laws. For the same God who said, 'You must not commit adultery,' also said, 'You must not murder.' So if you murder someone, but do not commit adultery, you have still broken the law. So whatever you say or whatever you do, remember that you will be judged by the law that sets you free. There will be no mercy for those who have not shown mercy to others. But if you have been merciful, God will be merciful when he judges you. (NLT)

When you show partiality to anyone for their externals (dress, social standing, race, tattoos, piercings) you commit a sin. Let me give you an example. There was a time in my life when I'd judge on appearance alone. If I saw a homeless woman come by, I would be inclined to give her money, food, whatever. But if a homeless man came by, and he had body piercing and tattoos, I would say to myself, "I'm not giving him money, he'll spend it on drugs or booze." What did I just do? I judged one worthy and the other unworthy because of externals. But if I show mercy to both, without reservation, when the Lord looks at my life He will give back to me the measure of mercy I gave to others. Mercy will cancel out areas where I have missed the mark (Matthew 5:7; 7:2; Luke 6:37).

A MATTER OF CITIZENSHIP

Maybe this last example will help you. Luke 16:16 says, *"The law and the prophets were until John. Since that time the kingdom of God has been preached, and everyone is pressing into it."* There is a transfer of kingdoms taking place in that statement. When I was growing up, communism was prevalent in many areas of the world. There was something called the Berlin Wall. It was a man-made structure that had staunch military enforcement if you tried to pass either way through that wall. Once in a while someone would find a way to escape the tyranny and risk their lives by sneaking over to West Berlin. Once they crossed over they were free, but they could never go back. They were fugitives and would be shot on sight if they returned.

That's sort of what this is like. Jesus is saying that you all were once citizens of this kingdom of the Law and Prophets but now you live in the kingdom of Graceland. And if you go back there, you'll be a fugitive of the law and be rightly judged as guilty.

Luke 6:35-37 adds:

> But love your enemies, do good, and lend, hoping for noth-
> ing in return; and your reward will be great, and you will
> be sons of the Most High. For He is kind to the unthankful
> and evil. Therefore be merciful, just as your Father also
> is merciful. "Judge not, and you shall not be judged. Con-
> demn not, and you shall not be condemned.

Did you get that? Like in football some of us catch the pass,
and then fumble it. What's He saying? The Father is kind to evil
men. Be like Him. These commands are not related to anyone
you would normally associate with or like. These are wicked, evil
people. Paul tells us that it's the kindness of God that leads to repentance. In the kingdom of the Law and Prophets you slay your
enemies. In the kingdom of Graceland you love them, and more
importantly you are kind to them.

John 20:19-23:

> That evening the disciples were meeting behind locked doors
> because they were afraid of the Jewish leaders. Suddenly, Jesus
> was standing there among them! 'Peace be with you,' he said.
> As he spoke, he showed them the wounds in his hands and
> his side. They were filled with joy when they saw the Lord!
> Again he said, 'Peace be with you.' As the Father has sent me,
> so I am sending you." Then he breathed on them and said,
> 'Receive the Holy Spirit. If you forgive anyone's sins, they are
> forgiven. If you do not forgive them, they are not forgiven.

The commission to forgive sins is phrased in an unusual
manner. Literally in the Greek it is: "Those whose sins you forgive have already been forgiven; those whose sins you do not forgive have not been forgiven." God does not forgive people's sins
because we decide to do so, nor does he withhold forgiveness
because we will not grant it. We announce it; we do not create it.

This is the essence of salvation. And all who proclaim the Gospel are in effect forgiving or not forgiving sins, depending on whether the hearer accepts or rejects the Lord Jesus as the *Sin-Bearer*. A very prominent leader in the Body of Christ put it this way:[4]

- Mercy withholds the knife from the heart of Isaac;
- Grace provides a ram in the thicket (Genesis 22:11-14);
- Mercy runs to forgive the prodigal (Luke 15: 20-24);
- Grace throws a party with a robe a ring and a fatted calf;
- Mercy hears a cry of the thief on the cross (Luke 23:20-24);
- Grace promises paradise that very day;
- Mercy converts Saul on the road to Damascus (Acts 9: 1-6);
- Grace calls him to be a great apostle;
- Mercy closes the door to hell (Ephesians 2:8-9);
- Grace opens the door to heaven.

And the difference between mercy and grace is this - mercy withholds from us what we deserve. Grace gives us what we do not deserve.

BREAKING THE FOUR MINUTE MILE

I realize the above subtitle might mean something to the baby boomer generation, but to most everyone else it doesn't. There was something called the "four minute mile" that was considered a barrier that would probably never be broken by humans running in such a race. There was even scientific thought that said that the human body was incapable of propelling itself fast enough over the length of one mile to break that barrier.

In 1952 Roger Bannister broke that barrier and became an instant hero worldwide. Since that time, men have actually shaved almost seventeen seconds off that record. That's a lot of time, relatively speaking. Hold that thought for a few minutes as we unwrap this next part.

2 Corinthians 5:17-20 says:

Therefore, if anyone is in Christ, he is a new creation; old things have passed away; behold, all things have become new. Now all things are of God, who has reconciled us to Himself through Jesus Christ, and has given us the ministry of reconciliation, that is, that God was in Christ reconciling the world to Himself, not counting their trespasses against them, and has committed to us the ministry of reconciliation. We are therefore Christ's ambassadors, as though God were making His appeal through us.

What is our ministry according to the above Corinthian quote? Before you answer that, let me give you some hints. This is not a ministry for the five-fold or deacons and elders.

Ephesians 4:11-12 reads:

And He Himself gave some to be apostles, some prophets, some evangelists, and some pastors and teachers, for the equipping of the saints for the work of ministry, for the edifying of the body of Christ.

Paul was addressing the church at large. So everyone reading this has at least one ministry in common. You have the ministry of reconciliation. What does that mean? It means that you don't count people's transgression against them because He doesn't. You are an ambassador of that message. Are you doing your job?

Usually the last thing sinners want to hear is that they are sinners. They already know that. It is the Holy Spirit's job to convict them of sin. Your job is to say, "Hey, I have incredible news for you. God wants to take all the thousands of bad things you have done and completely delete them." What does that look like? Well over the years I have had moments with my computers when I have spent two or three days typing out my notes for a sermon and somehow inadvertently forget to save the changes when I close out the document. And instantly there is this rush of panic and then angst. I could send my computer to Bill Gates and even he isn't going to be able to recover that information. It's gone forever.

That's what Paul is saying here. You and I can share that same type of message about people's sins being lost forever. God is telling me to tell them that He will not count their transgression against them. How? When they come to Christ.

Chapter 3 | OUR IDENTITY

WHO ARE YOU?

Then God saw everything that He had made, and indeed it was very good. So the evening and the morning were the sixth day.

Genesis 1:31

This is the first creation. Everything is good. So what started very good eventually became very corrupt. Why? Because of sin.

Also, Hebrews 8:7-13 says,

For if that first covenant had been faultless, then no place would have been sought for a second. Because finding fault with them, He says "Behold, the days are coming, says the Lord, when I will make a new covenant with the house of Israel and with the house of Judah - not according to the covenant that I made with their fathers in the day when I took them by the hand to lead them out of the land of Egypt; because they did not continue in My covenant, and I disregarded them, says the Lord. For this is the covenant that I will make with the house of Israel after those days, says the Lord: I will put My laws in their mind and write them on their hearts; and I will be their God, and they shall be My people. None of them shall teach his neighbor, and none his brother, saying, 'Know the Lord,' for all shall know Me, from the least of them to the greatest of them. For I will be merciful to their unrighteousness, and their sins and their lawless deeds I will remember no more.

Remember what we read in 2 Corinthians 5:

In that He says, 'A new covenant.' He has made the first obsolete. Now what is becoming obsolete and growing old is ready to vanish away.

The first covenant required human effort to fulfill but with no power to do it. The second covenant gave us a new nature and the power of grace to live it out. Jesus is the only human who can ever claim "self-righteousness." Why? Because He never sinned.

Over the years I have heard people say things like, "Yes, I am saved but I realize I have a sin nature and I mess up a lot." Some of you have probably said similar things. What that eventually leads to is a "qué será será" attitude or "whatever will be, will be." But that's not what the scripture says. Earlier we read the numerous times Paul called the church saints, and you can't be a sinner and a saint at the same time. If you are a sinner that means if we leave you alone for very long you will mess up.

There was a time in my pastoral life when I would counsel someone and listen as he would tell me about patterns of sin and show frustration. I would affirm his sin nature and agree that things will happen to veer him off course. But I was wrong in my thinking. Does the Bible say that, "If anyone is in Christ he or she has a sin nature"? No. If I tell you that, then I should not be surprised if you go out and continue to sin because you are only fulfilling what I told you.

If you tell people they are sinners, they will sin by faith. It's another example of lowering the value of scripture to the level of my experience. I may feel like a sinner because of struggles I am facing with past sin issues. However, it's in the struggle we exercise our faith.

In Hebrews 11:1 it say:

Faith is the substance of things hoped for, the evidence of things not seen." The Amplified Bible will help with this im-

*portant matter with wording it says, "Now faith is the as-
surance (the confirmation, the title deed) of the things [we]
hope for, being the proof of things [we] do not see and the
conviction of their reality [faith perceiving as real fact what
is not revealed to the senses].*

This flaw is often found in the theology of healing. It most
often happens like this, if we pray for people and they are not
healed, we formulate a doctrine that says God doesn't heal anymore and disregard what Jesus said and did. In simple terms,
this means that you can read the Bible and change your understanding of it by your experience or lack thereof. It comes down
to faith. When we believe God there is a new highway that opens
up in your life. It is a highway of holiness, a highway of righteousness.

So are you telling me that when I became a Christian I'm no
longer supposed to sin? No that's not what I am telling you. That
is what the Bible says. Hold that thought. Remember my example of Roger Banister? Once he broke the four minute mile from
that point on, runners were breaking it all the time. Why? In part
because they believed they could.

If I keep teaching you that you have a sin nature after salvation in Christ, you in a sense won't break the four minute mile.
Well what happens when I tell you that you are a saint and you
happen to sin? You have a lawyer to defend you. Jesus is called
our High Priest forever. He is there to apply the mercy and grace
you require to move past sin and on to restoration. You say I
have a problem with pornography, lying, gluttony, etc. Let's look
at that.

BAD FLESH VS. GOOD FLESH

There are certain words that often trigger negative connota-
tions within The Church. The word "flesh" has such tension. Bad
flesh or *sarx* (from the Greek) denotes mere human nature, the
earthly nature of man apart from divine influence, and therefore

prone to sin and opposed to God"

I want to give you an illustration of the bad flesh in nature. There is a medical or pathological condition known as "proud flesh." It is most common in horses and other animals, but can occur in humans. When a wound occurs, instead of it healing correctly something called "proud flesh" grows rapidly over the wound and can give the appearance of healing when it is simply covering up an infected area. One experienced horse owner said this, "If you ever get proud flesh you will know it by its rotten odor. Just like when a person gets a bad wound and does not go to the doctor, the flesh can die, and the tissues underneath seem not to heal."

Usually when that occurs, the veterinarian has to surgically remove the proud flesh and re-dress the wound to keep it clean so it can grow good flesh. Removing that proud flesh causes it to die.

In a manner of speaking, before Christ you were proud flesh. You looked wholesome, but underneath everything was rotten to the core. That's why Paul said in my flesh dwells no good thing. But throughout the New Testament Paul says that when you were born again all of that proud flesh died. It was circumcised or cut away.

John 1 says, "The Word became flesh and dwelt among us." Who is John talking about? Jesus. So if the human flesh is inherently evil, Jesus, being of human flesh, was evil by nature. But the opposite is true. Jesus was tempted in every way like us, yet, was without sin.

Hebrews 4:14,15:

Seeing then that we have a great High Priest who has passed through the heavens, Jesus the Son of God, let us hold fast our confession. For we do not have a High Priest who cannot sympathize with our weaknesses, but was in all points tempted as we are, yet without sin.

And again Galatians 2:20 says:

I have been crucified with Christ; it is no longer I who live, but Christ lives in me; and the life which I now live in the flesh I live by faith in the Son of God, who loved me and gave Himself for me.

So there is bad flesh and good flesh. The transition from one to the other is by faith. Like the four minute mile, if you don't believe you can run it…guess what…you won't.

1 John 3:4-9 says:

"Everyone who practices sin also practices lawlessness; and sin is lawlessness. You know that He appeared in order to take away sins; and in Him there is no sin. No one who abides in Him sins; no one who sins has seen Him or knows Him. Little children, make sure no one deceives you; the one who practices righteousness is righteous, just as He is righteous; the one who practices sin is of the devil; for the devil has sinned from the beginning The Son of God appeared for this purpose, to destroy the works of the devil. No one who is born of God practices sin, because His seed abides in him; and he cannot sin, because he is born of God." (NAS)

Yikes Batman, which one is it? Both. There is this divine tension going on in all of us. Verses taken literally and out of context can torment you. But in chapter two John says if you do sin you have a lawyer who can get you acquitted, not because He makes deals with other lawyers, but because He has access to a well of mercy and grace that He has paid for. The point is that you are not supposed to be practicing sin. Why? Because you have a new nature.

If someone told you that after you were born again you were still going to sin a lot and don't worry about it, that would be like telling people they can't break the four minute mile. It's not imparting the faith you need or the promise of power to change your spiritual atmosphere. Can you live perfectly? You can. Will you? Probably not. But here is the key. Sin used to be the rule, not the exception. Now not sinning is the rule, and sin is an exception. We must create a culture where people expect to live without sin. If you do that you will run a lot faster because you believe you can break a barrier no one thought was possible.

WHO ARE YOU?

Has it ever dawned on you that if we think correctly about God we will think correctly about ourselves and each other? In Matthew 16:13-18 Jesus asked two very important questions that are still every bit as important today. The first was "who do men say that I am?" The second question was aimed at His twelve; "OK…now who do **you** say that I am? The answer to that question became and still is today the greatest question any human being can address. Our eternity hangs in the balance.

A third question I would like to ask you is… "Who are you?" I don't mean what it says on your driver's license. That really isn't your identity. That's the name your parents gave you when you were born but that's not really who you are. There are things that are true but there are things that are more true. For example, my name is David, that is true but what is more true is what God says about me. It requires a renewed mind to sort it out and make it real. When Jesus asked, "Who do men say that I am" their answers were true. He was doing things that the prophets of old did like Elijah, Jeremiah. But what was more true, was the fact that He was called the only begotten Son by His Father. That was and is who He is.

Romans 12:2 says:

And do not be conformed to this world, but be transformed by the renewing of your mind, that you may prove what is that good and acceptable and perfect will of God. For I say, through the grace given to me, to everyone who is among you, not to think of himself more highly than he ought to think, but to think soberly, as God has dealt to each one a measure of faith. For as we have many members in one body, but all the members do not have the same function, so we, being many, are one body in Christ, and individually members of one another. Having then gifts differing according to the grace that is given to us, let us use them: if prophecy, let us prophesy in proportion to our faith; or ministry, let us use it in our ministering; he who teaches, in teaching; he who exhorts, in exhortation; he who gives, with liberality; he who leads, with diligence; he who shows mercy, with cheerfulness.

Paul is saying that you know you are being conformed to this world not by how much TV you watch or video games you play (though that could be a problem) but when you don't value people who are not like you. Being conformed to this world starts with "thinking more highly of himself than he ought to." Paul is not saying to think of yourself as lowly and insignificant.

In my Strength Finders life coaching experience a few years ago I discovered that the two most important things in life are that you know God and that you know you; in that order. When you require people to lose their identity and become like you that's called control. Paul calls it conformity. When you're transformed you value people who are different than you.

So that's the context but the principle is the same for other Kingdom realms. We are supposed to be in a continual state of transformation because many of our presuppositions in life must be replaced with Kingdom thinking. Luke 2:52 says, "And Jesus increased in wisdom and stature, and in favor with God and men." Jesus wasn't born preprogrammed with Kingdom thinking. He had to grow into His destiny. When Jesus called the Twelve to be with Him eventually they were called apostles because they became transformed delegates of another world. Jesus had to get them to a place of surrender so He could trust them with further understanding.

An unsurrendered heart will reject many things in the Kingdom because they conflict with your conditioned way of thinking. In **2 Corinthians 3:16** it says that when Hebrews believed the veil was lifted. That's really important to get that. It didn't say when the veil was lifted then they believed. It tells me that my heart is able to capture things my mind does not understand. But even to this day, when Moses is read, a veil lies on their heart. Nevertheless when one turns to the Lord, the veil is taken away. (2 Corinthians 3:15-16)

The Lord gives revelation to those that have already said yes in their heart.

1 Peter 1 says:

Grace and peace be multiplied to you in the knowledge of God and of Jesus our Lord, as His divine <u>power has given to us all things that pertain to life and godliness, through the knowledge of Him</u> who called us by glory and virtue."

For me that means there is untold power available at all times but it just doesn't happen because it's true. It happens because you've said "Amen.

The word "Amen" makes its first appearance in the Bible under the most serious circumstances. When a husband accused his wife of adultery, and she protested her innocence, the matter was settled by God under the test of bitter water (Numbers 5:12-31). The woman was taken to the priest and the priest put her under oath. She submitted to a ceremony in which she drank some water containing dust from the tabernacle floor. If she had committed adultery she was to be cursed with a wasting disease. But if she did not get sick then she was proven innocent and her husband was proven wrong.

During the ceremony, when the priest pronounced the curse, the woman was required by God to say, "Amen, Amen". (Numbers

5:22). That is the first occurrence of the word in scripture. The Lord commands it to be said by a person who is yielding herself to examination by Him in His Presence. In other words she welcomed God's outcome wholeheartedly and without hesitation.

So then, in 2 Corinthians 1:20:

For all the promises of God in Him are Yes...

Jesus is the Divine "Yes" and we are the "Amen". Everything you will ever need is already stored up for you in God. Jesus comes along and says I am the "Yes" of God. You and I are the "Amen". That means I am not just glibly confessing God's promises in my life but I am yielding to Him without limits even before I know what it is I am saying Amen to. That is unAmerican! We are taught to read the fine print before ever agreeing to the terms.

Romans 6:3-9:

Or do you not know that as many of us as were baptized into Christ Jesus were baptized into His death? Therefore we were buried with Him through baptism into death, that just as Christ was raised from the dead by the glory of the Father, even so we also should walk in newness of life. For if we have been united together in the likeness of His death, certainly we also shall be in the likeness of His resurrection, knowing this, that our old man was crucified with Him, that the body of sin might be done away with, that we should no longer be slaves of sin. For he who has died has been freed from sin. Now if we died with Christ, we believe that we shall also live with Him, knowing that Christ, having been raised from the dead, dies no more. Death no longer has dominion over Him. For the death that He died, He died to sin once for all; but the life that He lives, He lives to God.

Paul uses water baptism to illustrate this powerful truth. He is therefore declaring that baptism is not symbolic but prophetic. It identifies your new life with a future full of faith and freedom. This means that this act is supposed to recalibrate our lives as it pertains to our capacity to sin.

Romans 6:11 says it like this:

Likewise you also, reckon yourselves to be dead indeed to sin.

Someone said it's like a third shoe. You don't have a foot to put it on. This means it is supposed to become so real to you that if the enemy comes by and brings up your past…you can say " ya…well that dude is dead". That is more than a cute illustration. It is Heaven's "yes"…and you're "Amen".

The scripture says it's dead…not dying…but dead. It doesn't mean I have lost the capacity to sin. It's now not who I am. Stop giving your Amen to a lie that says you are just a sinner saved by grace trying to keep your head above water till you get to Heaven. That is what I hear many Christians say. Stop it!

Did you know that animals like cows chew the cud more than once? Many times they lack the digestive enzymes to break down certain things they eat so they bring it back up and chew it again so that it can be more readily digested in their stomach. This holds true with meditating on God's word. We keep bringing it up over and over again until it becomes part of our makeup.

Mary is a good example. She had promises given to her about her firstborn Son. For thirty years, she meditated, chewing and re-chewing the promises of God. Then in John 2 she is with close friends at a wedding when they ran out of wine. Something inside Mary said that Jesus could fix this problem very simply so she brings it up to her Son Jesus. His response appears to be a rebuke. "It's not yet my time". Imagine this with me if you're a mom. Picture your son who you birthed, who you raised, who you nurtured, knowing what God told you about Him; telling you to cool your jets because it's not time. I think she didn't look at the servants when she said "do whatever he tells you". I think she looked at Jesus with the eyes only a mama can give. Eyes that would stare at Him and say, "I know who you are." She would not be ignored.

I believe that Mary pondered and mediated and chewed over and over the promises of God in her life. Her mind went from the wonder of God's promise as a pregnant teenager to the surety of His word because Mary's mind was renewed. It really starts there for us as well.

If I were to ask you again "who are you" your answer should be something like: "I am a son / daughter of God. He has given me all that I need to live Godly all the days of my life". "I am not a sinner…I am a saint". When you do that you may be calling that which is not as though it is and in doing that you give yourself time to chew the cud over and over until it is digested and becomes a part of who you are.

If we've left the country where sin is sovereign, how can we still live in our old house there? Or didn't you realize we packed up and left there for good? That is what happened in baptism. When we went under the water, we left the old country of sin behind; when we came up out of the water, we entered into the new country of grace—a new life in a new land!

That's what baptism into the life of Jesus means. When we are lowered into the water, it is like the burial of Jesus; when we are raised up out of the water, it is like the resurrection of Jesus. Each of us is raised into a light-filled world by our Father so that we can see where we're going in our new grace-sovereign country.

Could it be any clearer? Our old way of life was nailed to the cross with Christ, a decisive end to that sin-miserable life—no longer at sin's every beck and call! What we believe is this: If we get included in Christ's sin-conquering death, we also get included in his life-saving resurrection. Romans 6:6-11 Message Bible

Think of this way….sin speaks a language you no longer understand. God speaks your mother tongue and it's the only language you know. You do not wrestle against flesh & blood. Dead people don't wrestle and they don't fight. We don't battle against an old nature. It's dead. It's a fight against an enemy who is real and unrelenting. They are not creative they mimic your old nature. You feel this pull and that is not your old nature it's a lie crouching at the door to get in.

GRACELAND: WHAT DOES IT LOOK LIKE?

There is really no end to the possibilities of covering the issues of grace in the Kingdom. Do you know that there will come a day when grace will no longer be necessary.

2 Corinthians 12:9-10 says:

And He said to me, 'My grace is sufficient for you, for My strength is made <u>perfect</u> in weakness.' Therefore most gladly I will rather boast in my infirmities, that the power of Christ may rest upon me. Therefore I take pleasure in infirmities, in reproaches, in needs, in persecutions, in distresses, for Christ's sake. For when I am weak, then I am strong.

Perfect is a powerful concept. In John 19:30 Jesus drank the vinegar and said, *"It is finished."* All of the grace you will ever need has been paid in full at Calvary. Maybe you thought He only died for your sin. Actually what He paid for will allow you to have Him become strong in your weakness.

Some time ago I heard a story about some Italian immigrants. Back in the early 20th century a large family decided to save money and come to America through Ellis Island. They purchased a one way ticket on a large cruise ship, and once on board they thought they needed to save as much money as possible so they could begin a new life here in the United States.

Knowing that the voyage would take about three weeks, they packed many helpings of crackers and cheese for their meager, but life-sustaining meals. Finally, the night before they arrived in New York City the captain announced that they would dock in the harbor the next day. Needless to say, the family rejoiced. So the patriarch of the family decided this was one occasion that was so important they would celebrate it with a full meal in the dining hall. When he went to inquire about the cost of the meal for his large family, the steward was stunned. He commented that he didn't understand why the man was asking such a thing because the meals in the dining hall were covered in the price of the tickets for the voyage.

For three weeks this man and his whole family ate crackers and cheese when they could have dined with all of the guests at the banquet table. That is often the picture of the church. I believe many of us have settled for cheese and crackers when we have been invited to the banquet hall.

What Jesus paid for was a complete package. It is so complete that it is intended to lavish us as long as we are in this body. If the family that ate cheese and crackers for three weeks knew that they could have had T-bone steaks and prime rib what do you think they would have chosen? When I live under the cloud of guilt for bad decisions, sometimes not even morally wrong, it's almost as if I choose to eat crackers and cheese. This occurs because we have convinced ourselves that grace is reserved for special people and we need to stay humble with cheese and crackers.

When you come to the banquet table and feast with others guests because you no longer have to eat cheese and crackers, the one who paid for the banquet is honored. "I am humbled because he gave me a seat at the table."

It's much much more difficult to receive what you don't deserve than it is to receive what you deserve. And when I allow that to happen, the One who gave it is honored.

Today we are facing an unprecedented crisis (at least in my lifetime) in the world financial markets. Even committed Christians are reeling. How does that happen? Let's say that I know there's a good chance the Buffalo Bills may get in the Super Bowl this year so I buy a high definition 3D Plasma Screen television. And all the while I am thinking about this being a blessing from the Lord. And after it's all installed, the Bills don't even get in the playoffs (I'm not prophesying that ☺).

I'm disappointed; but that's just the start. As the payments for this system start coming, I realize I just committed to something that is going to severely challenge my finances. In addition, it will disrupt the peace of my life and my household. Not long into this nightmare it becomes apparent to me that this probably was not a blessing from the Lord, but a consequence of my greed.

So I have the joy of enduring 48 months of payments and the television will probably end up costing me three times what it was originally worth. So when I get alone with God I realize I have sinned. I know in my heart I have taken resources He has entrusted me with and just fed a sector of the American economy that is built on poor saps like me. And I tell Him from my heart...I am truly sorry. Not because I have to bare this horrible burden for 48 months, but because I have misused His resources. When I come to that place of brokenness He does forgive me.

But still I have this monthly agony I forced upon myself thinking somehow it will build humility in me. This is the woe is me kind of mindset. It may shock some of you, but the reality is that when Jesus said, "It is finished," He not only bought me, He bought my problems. I don't have to go through this alone. It is no longer my problem, but now it's our problem. There was a time when God literally wiped away a $30,000-plus debt that was a result of greed-driven business decisions in my BC days. There were other things along that journey He did not wipe out and I had to pay them off by selling my 1962 Corvette and other things to pay bills. When my wife Lisa married me she got a real bad deal by worldly standards, at least that is what I thought. But thank God there was Graceland.

CHAPTER 4 | A JUST VIEW OF JUSTICE

WHAT OF JUSTICE?

Biblical justice has a different standard. Isaiah 61 says Jesus came to "free the captive." Let's be honest here. The prisoner is probably in there because he did something dumb. True biblical justice works like this. Once a person is truly converted, biblical justice is no longer aimed at the person who did something wrong, but it is now aimed at the thing behind that foolish act that caused him to mess up. It's no longer aimed at the sinner, but the power that influenced him; more specifically, the powers of hell that enchanted him into greed.

The reproach of your actions is not supposed to be an issue any longer. Once the blood of Jesus washed you, you can't get any cleaner.[7] That's why early on in this book we declared that you are no longer a sinner but a saint. It has been said that He doesn't take away your ability to sin. He takes away your ability to enjoy it. Malachi 3:16 says, *"Then those who feared the Lord spoke to one another, and the Lord listened and heard them; so a book of remembrance was written before Him for those who fear the Lord and who meditate on His name."* Have you ever wondered how Malachi received this revelation? Did you notice it doesn't name names?

It doesn't say Abraham, Isaac, Jacob, Moses, Joseph, etc. Rather, these are everyday folks like you and me. Not superstars, just saints. Some of you reading this book have had a real bummer of a week. Sometimes I remind our people on Sunday morning, "As soon as the music started you didn't stand there and wait for the worship team to play a song you liked, you determined in your heart that no matter how you felt you were going to proclaim with your mouth how wonderful He is. In the midst of real struggle, you proclaimed how good He is."

You will never be able to offer that kind of sacrifice again. Once you are in Heaven there will be no brokenness or struggle. And when you offer real worship, He listens. He makes sure every word is recorded. I find that amazing!

Genesis 18:9-15 says:

> *Then they said to him, 'Where is Sarah your wife?' So he said, 'Here, in the tent.' And He said, 'I will certainly return to you according to the time of life, and behold, Sarah your wife shall have a son." (Sarah was listening in the tent door which was behind him.) "Now Abraham and Sarah were old, well advanced in age; and Sarah had passed the age of childbearing. Therefore Sarah laughed within herself, saying, 'After I have grown old, shall I have pleasure, my lord being old also?' And the Lord said to Abraham, 'Why did Sarah laugh, saying, 'Shall I surely bear a child, since I am old?' Is anything too hard for the Lord? At the appointed time I will return to you, according to the time of life, and Sarah shall have a son.' But Sarah denied it, saying, 'I did not laugh,' for she was afraid. And He said, 'No, but you did laugh!'*

Now look at what it says in Hebrews 11:11:

> *By faith Sarah herself also received strength to conceive seed, and she bore a child when she was past the age, because she judged Him faithful who had promised.*

What just happened here? I think the first part was written for the original reader, and the second was written for us. I can identify with Genesis 18. God chooses to remember that His grace restores us. Grace looks to "find the gold" in your life and when He finds it, He remembers and records it. Sarah mocked God by laughing at Him, then she lied about it. Many of us would be upset with ourselves in similar situations. But at one point Sarah believes God's promise and that is what He chooses to record about her and about you! Are you glad about this?

Is God honored when I live under the burden of the things I did wrong yesterday or last year? I was thinking about the more than 50 million babies that have been aborted since Roe vs. Wade. No one knows for sure, but there are probably 30 to 40 million moms who are still alive that carry the anguish of that act. Many have come to Him and repented. And when that happens He is delighted. He surely says to the recording angel something like, "Look she did it. She turned to me…she's come to me in brokenness…that's my girl…she is amazing. Write that down!" When that mom crosses over, I believe the Father will have the son or daughter who was aborted waiting for that mom or dad to escort them into glory. He's that kind of Father.

I dishonor the grace of God by thinking that living under a cloud of regret and fear will keep me humble.

Are there things I would do differently now than I did in the past? Oh boy, you bet, too many to recount. But I can't live there because it will rob me of the life He has paid for. According to the book my Father has, I am celebrated by Him as a son. And He is proud of me.

TRUTH, JUSTICE AND THE AMERICAN WAY

We had Paul Manwaring from Bethel church with us some time ago, and he said some things that stirred my heart and provoked me to dig deeper into the meaning of justice. It's sometimes like trying to hit a moving target because the concept of justice can be extremely subjective. We as a nation have prided ourselves on "truth, justice and the American way." Some people think this is in our constitution.

On the website, *www.simplemarriage.net*, there was an interesting quote that read, "For millennia philosophers have debated this question. Justice, like beauty or goodness, is an ethereal and hard to define concept. Catholic theologian and philosopher St.

Thomas Aquinas put it quite succinctly when he defined justice as the constant and perpetual will to render to everyone his due. I think it's the same idea of justice that Benjamin Franklin had. Those who uphold the laws, rules and standards are rewarded. Those who do not are punished. Injustice occurs when a man denies an individual or group either the punishment or reward due them."[8]

The interesting thing is that the scriptures clearly indicate God loves justice; however I don't think it's at this level of human need. Back in the '90s, a man I saw on many Sundays run the football for the Buffalo Bills, was indicted for the gruesome murder of his ex-wife and her friend. Many people, including his former in-laws, were outraged that he was acquitted. To this day, those former in-laws may be full of bitterness because of the injustice they feel in their lives. That story repeats itself millions of times in our history.

As I sat in our sanctuary listening to Paul make comments on justice, it began to provoke me to go deeper. Eventually it ministered to my soul. You see I have preached messages about justice that pertain to the very nature of God. The Bible says that the foundation of His throne is justice and righteousness. We as Christians must be very careful about demanding justice in our lives because we can step into an arena the enemy thrives in, and it can bring nasty repercussions upon us.

However, I realize that the kind of justice God seems to revel in the most has little to do with payback and punishment. In 1 Kings 3:16-28 Solomon is given any wish he desires by God. He chooses wisdom above all things available to him. And we find in the very next scene two prostitutes who give birth to babies in the span of three days. Apparently, they live in some kind of brothel together. As the story is recorded, one woman wakes up to find that her baby died apparently because he or she suffocated from the mom lying on him or her all night.

Out of desperation and hopelessness she switches babies while the other woman is sleeping. Upon awakening, the betrayed mother realizes that the dead baby lying next to her is not her child, but the baby with the other woman is hers. Both women are forced to go to Solomon to cast judgment on the situation.

In the opening of the trial Solomon doesn't ask for evidence or a witness. In that day there was no such thing as fingerprints or DNA testing. He goes right to the heart of matter. Solomon ordered that the baby be cut in two, and half be given to each mother. He knows the real mother of the child will do anything to preserve life, even if it means giving that child up. She could bear that heartache, the other she could not. That's exactly what happened.

1 Kings 3:28 says:

"When all Israel heard the verdict the king had given, they held the king in awe, because they saw that he had wisdom from God to administer justice.

But wait a minute. Wouldn't you think justice would have included arresting that other woman for kidnapping? That's not what happens here. Justice was served, at least in Solomon's mind, when the relationship between the mother and her baby was restored. That was justice.

Psalm 89:14 adds:

Righteousness and justice are the foundation of your throne; love and faithfulness go before you.

This is the same God who desires that none should perish, but that all should come to repentance. God's heart is not that sinners receive the just reward for their sins, but rather that He be restored to the children who were taken from Him after Adam's sin in the garden.[9]

This kind of justice is the same kind Solomon released upon the woman who pleaded for the life of her baby. It flies in the face of my narrow American thinking that people who do really bad things deserve to be brought to justice. Romans 13 clearly bears that out. But if that is all justice is to us, I believe we miss the facet of justice I call…Kingdom Justice. It can only come out of heaven's perspective. Solomon had heaven's perspective.

Isaiah 9:7 says:

Of the increase of His government and peace there will be no end, upon the throne of David and over His kingdom, to order it and establish it with judgment and justice from that time forward, even forever.

This justice is not the cry of retribution, revenge or the balancing of scales. It is not the satisfaction that someone got their just dues and therefore you feel better about being wronged. That's the world's justice not Kingdom justice. There was a season of my life when I would cry out for justice for the children slaughtered in abortions. I still do, but now my heart for justice wants to see the baby have a relationship with the parents. The act of taking the baby's life severs all hope of relationship in a moment of time. The cry should be to allow that baby to have a lifelong relationship with his or her natural parents, or with another mother and father waiting in the wings to adopt that child for life. That's Kingdom justice.

That is what happened when Solomon issued his justice. People heard of it and said, "This man is amazing." Why? Because they had been introduced to Kingdom justice and they had no grid for it. All they understood was The Law. Today, if the world hears you cry out for justice for babies being aborted, it implies to them that we are condemning the mother.

I'm drawn to FBI-type shows because my heart is always on a quest for justice. Sometimes the show will end and the sentence seems too light to me, or may even end with a hung jury, and I'm conflicted inside because my flesh cries out for justice. Kingdom justice is when the blood touches the offense. Not the blood of the criminal, but the blood of Jesus. When that touches the offense, Kingdom justice is released in a way that no earthy court can compete with it.

I've watched situation after situation where someone sees a criminal prosecuted for killing a loved one, and sometimes the punishment might even be the death penalty. Many times when they interview the offended party they will say things like, "I'm glad that justice was carried out, but it doesn't touch the loss I feel." Human blood cannot satisfy the heartache of a person who had a loved one murdered.

The cry for justice has been voiced through American heroes like Dr. Martin Luther King, Jr. who said,

> I have a dream that one day, down in Alabama, with its vicious racists, with its governor having his lips dripping with the words of 'interposition' and 'nullification' -- one day right there in Alabama little black boys and black girls will be able to join hands with little white boys and white girls as sisters and brothers.

The cry of this great hero was one for justice that would restore relationships between Caucasians and African Americans. King went on to say,

> I have a dream today! I have a dream that one day every valley shall be exalted, and every hill and mountain shall be made low, the rough places will be made plain, and the crooked places will be made straight; and the glory of the Lord shall be revealed and all flesh shall see it together.

It's about restoring men back to the dignity that comes from our Creator. It's about relational restoration. He added,

> And when this happens, when we allow freedom to ring, when we let it ring from every village and every hamlet, from every state and every city, we will be able to speed up that day when all of God's children, black men and

white men, Jews and Gentiles, Protestants and Catholics, will be able to join hands and sing in the words of the old Negro spiritual: Free at last! Free at last! Thank God Almighty, we are free at last![10]

The challenge to us is to examine our hearts about this American dream of justice versus Kingdom justice. One is superior to the other. I'm not suggesting we throw out our judicial system. That is way beyond my capacity to comprehend.

Paul Manwaring tells a wonderful story about Kingdom Justice. He was a prison warden and he shared a story about a prison in Sugarland, Texas with a ministry led by Chuck Colson and Prison Fellowship that leads men to Christ while incarcerated. There was an inmate there for murdering a young woman. The young woman's mother's name is Mrs. Washington, and her daughter was killed in a drug raid that went bad. Sometime later Mrs. Washington's husband suffered a stroke and died because of the trauma of losing his daughter. Shortly after that her son died of AIDS, contracted while doing drugs that he began taking after the murder of his sister. It was a horrible mess.

In an interesting turn of events, Mrs. Washington's pastor decided he would participate in a program within the prison to help facilitate reconciliation between prisoners and the people they committed crimes against. When Mrs. Washington heard that her pastor was doing this work she whimsically said, "If you see Ron Flowers (the man who killed her daughter) let me know." Well, you guessed it, he did indeed find Ron Flowers there. Ron had become a Christian in prison. Before that time, he denied his crime for 13 years. But after his conversion, he wrote a letter to Mrs. Washington and confessed.

After the exchange of letters, Mrs. Washington visited Ron Flowers in prison. As they sat across a table, this stately African American woman watched as Ron Flowers sobbed over the murder of her daughter. Eventually he was able to explain that she was not involved in drugs, but was simply at the wrong place, at the wrong time with a boyfriend who had gone bad.

As time went on Mrs. Washington began a relationship with Ron Flowers that blossomed from her willingness to forgive him. Then Chuck Colson came to assist in the graduation of inmates who participated in the program. Before Chuck Colson could hand Ron his certificate, Mrs. Washington walked up to a microphone and said, "Ron Flowers…if you will leave this prison and love the Lord your God and bring your children up to love God and love your wife…then I will adopt you as my son."

At that moment, 150 prisoners were crying as they watched Kingdom Justice take root in Ron Flowers and Mrs. Washington. Soon after that, Mrs. Washington received an anonymous check for $10,000 that she used to help Ron Flowers and his family get settled after his release. Every week, Ron Flowers visited his adopted mother. And Mrs. Washington later said that despite the pain and loss she suffered, this new-found son made it all worthwhile. This is true Kingdom justice. It has nothing to do with the twenty years Ron Flowers spent in jail.

What happened here is that the Blood touched the heart of offense of Mrs. Washington and released Kingdom Justice over a tragedy no human judicial system could touch. You cannot find that kind of justice in our courts because the courts are about the law. And they should be. But they have no power to release Kingdom justice because they are not designed to do that. What Jesus did on the cross fulfilled all that is required by our judicial system or any system of law for that matter.

In the Kingdom, the justice Jesus purchased is not just for the offender, but for the heart of the victim. Our cry for justice should be a cry for the Blood; not the blood of the offender who stole something from us, but the Blood of Jesus to come and touch that area that cannot be satisfied by earth-bound justice. It must be the release of Heaven's justice.

2 Corinthians 5:19 says:

That is, that God was in Christ reconciling the world to Himself, not imputing their trespasses to them, and has *committed to us the <u>word</u> of reconciliation.*

I believe that "word of reconciliation" is the word *justice*. (Jeremiah 9:24). My friend, Leif Hetland, noted that when Adam was created the first thing he saw was the face of God. The first thing he felt was the breath of God. The first thing he experienced was the pleasure of God. This is what was lost when Adam fell. When the Father put in motion a plan of justice it was to restore this very treasure He had with His first earthly son. When Heaven's justice is released upon us, we will once again see the face of God, experience the breath of God, and partake in the pleasure of His presence. I believe that is the loss God felt in the Garden as He was walking that fateful day and calling out for His son Adam.

CHAPTER 5 | TEACH US TO PRAY

KINGDOM POWER PRAYER

Now it came to pass, as He was praying in a certain place, when He ceased, that one of His disciples said to Him, "Lord, teach us to pray, as John also taught his disciples."

Luke 11:1

We don't know the exact chronology of this scene, but at this juncture of Jesus' ministry his disciples had been with Him long enough to see blind eyes and deaf ears opened, leprosy healed and the dead raised. The chapter before this in Luke the disciples had cast out devils and were all fired up.

I wish Luke had told us who asked this question, but as best we know it was one of the seventy followers. Personally, I think it was Peter. In any case, it appears at this point the atmosphere was right for a request to be made. It reminds me of the moment Solomon had when God appeared to him to ask, what is the "one" thing he would like.

Many of us today would have asked for more authority, power or position but this disciple saw something in Jesus' life that seemed to be the "one" thing that helped define His life, not just His ministry.

They were able to see everything Jesus did distilled down to "one" thing - His prayer life. With Jesus they spent their days ministering to people and weariness overcame Jesus and his disciples. This is a tiredness that sleep nor rest will invigorate. It can only be remedied by the presence of God.

Luke 11:2-4 says:

So He said to them, 'When you pray, say: "Our Father in heaven, hallowed be Your name. Your kingdom come your will be done on earth as it is in heaven. Give us day by day

*our daily bread. And forgive us our sins, for we also forgive
everyone who is indebted to us. And do not lead us into
temptation, but deliver us from the evil one.*

This prayer is also mentioned in Matthew 6 and it is apparent
that He taught it to a different set of people because the last part
is not there. I am not going to cover all the possible points in this
model except to say that it is presented as a very simple way to
pray. Over the years I have seen new believers around seasoned
saints who pray really eloquent prayers. When you hear them
pray it's like a compact Bible study. Even worse, when they pray
it's like they are preaching a sermon. I am convinced that sometimes folks like that are not praying to move God, but to impress
the people hearing their prayers.

New believers hear this and say, "Boy I'm not sure I could
ever pray like that." My first point is don't do that ☺. Praying is
conversation with God. Let's pretend that my son Noah asked
me to go fishing. And he said it like this, "Oh Dad...my Dad...
take me fishing. Oh Dad...for you are the one who knows all
about fishing. I claim this promise to go fishing, Oh Dad...for
you alone, Oh Dad, are my Dad and Dad...Oh Dad...you have
all knowledge about fishing, Oh Dad...and Dad, Oh Dad...I ask
this in the name of David, Oh Dad ☺."

It would be wrong for me to claim that people who pray in
this manner are not sincere and full of faith or that God will not
respond well to their prayers. That would be beside my point.
What is my point? Just talk natural. I don't think we would talk
to anyone else on the planet like that. The problem is somehow
we think God only listens to people who pray like that. Jesus de-
bunked that kind of prayer when He commented on the prayer
of the Pharisee against the prayer of a tax collector. Only one
walked away justified, and it wasn't the guy with the great religious prayer.

THE FORM

We can go to the other extreme and memorize words and recite them by rote with no heart. Jesus could have spent hours giving an amazing seminar on prayer, but He didn't. He gave them a form they could relate to at any level. And within this prayer are key areas that will either enhance or hinder it. One of them is dependence. He wants us never to forget that daily bread is something we must rely on Him for each day.

In Deuteronomy 8:17-18, God said:

Then you say in your heart, 'My power and the might of my hand have gained me this wealth.' And you shall remember the Lord your God, for it is He who gives you power to get wealth, that He may establish His covenant which He swore to your fathers, as it is this day.

The second thing is that forgiveness is critical. Just as bread is a daily need, so is forgiveness. We are called to be daily reconcilers, walking in a flow of forgiveness, so that the poison and bitterness of unforgiveness will not infect our lives.

PERSISTENT

In Luke 11:5-8 Jesus says:

And He said to them, 'Which of you shall have a friend, and go to him at midnight and say to him, 'Friend, lend me three loaves; for a friend of mine has come to me on his journey, and I have nothing to set before him'; and he will answer from within and say, 'Do not trouble me; the door is now shut, and my children are with me in bed; I cannot rise and give to you?' I say to you, though he will not rise and give to him because he is his friend, yet because of his persistence he will rise and give him as many as he needs.

Please understand this. Jesus just told them what to pray, but now He is about to tell them how to pray. Many times people separate this parable from the prayer He taught them. It goes together. Think of Him saying, "Since we are talking about prayer and you wanted me to teach you how to pray, listen carefully because this part is as important as the part I just told you. It's like a guy you know who has an unexpected friend come to his house late at night. He doesn't have any food, and even McDonald's is closed. So he knocks on your door and you say, 'I can't help right now. I'm in bed and I really don't want to disturb the whole house because all of my family is asleep.'"

Your friend answers by saying, "Wait, you don't understand, I need food for my guests and you are the only one who can help me right now. I'll return the food to you tomorrow when the market is open." He adds, "No...what is it about 'no' you don't understand?" He say, "Perhaps you didn't hear me, I have people in town who are hungry and I don't have food, but you do. I'll pay you back tomorrow!"

We don't know how long this goes on, but at one point the friend gave in just to get this guy off his back so he can get back to sleep. Jesus uses this as His focus of how to pray because He is highlighting real life in the natural, to teach them real life in the supernatural.

When we pray, keep it simple. We don't need a lot of religious rhetoric. You don't need to move the heart of God with your words - it was already moved when Jesus said, "It is finished." It's already in the contract. The covenant has already been made. Let's not get hung up on methods. If you are talking to the Father, and the prayer is supposed to go to the Son, please don't get hung up on that. He'll forward it to Jesus; the Father and the Son get along really well ☺.

In Luke 18, Jesus gives a similar example of a widow coming before an unrighteous judge who at first ignores her pleas. Eventually the judge gives her justice, not because he is just, but because he wants the woman off his back. She wore him out! What is Jesus telling us? He is explaining that when we pray, we put a bull's eye on a need. Persistence seems to be something Jesus is trying to emphasize. It's the one thing about prayer I don't like.

My last name in Italian means "now." Need I say anymore? It's as if my name is David Now. God's word completely contradicts my nature. Why? Because in the obedience of persistence guess who also gets changed? Me. You see, if you pray and pray and nothing happens in you, all you've had was a complaint session.

You can read all of the gospels and never once do you see someone come up to Jesus and say, "My son is tormented and throws himself in the fire," and Jesus responds, "I'm sorry. It must be his lot in life." Or a desperate father who begs Jesus to heal his daughter and he says, "Oh, it must be the Father's will for you to bear that cross." Not once!

Instead He is teaching us to say, "Hey I need your help. HELLO…excuse me…I've got the verse. I am asking you to do the same stuff that is consistent with what you did when you walked on this planet." Now that's a real prayer. In the process He is changing us. When we pray we are extending the Kingdom when that prayer is answered. We can't give up because there is resistance. Jesus said the violent take it by force. The violence referred to here is not a physical act of aggression against a perceived human enemy. It is rather a bold confident attitude that I can overcome resistance by the One who lives in me. I have been called to rule and reign, and wimpy people don't rule and reign very well.

In Luke 8, we read of the time Jesus gets into the boat with his disciples so they can get to the other side. Jesus goes down in a lower part of the boat and falls asleep. A really bad storm comes upon them and they are afraid, saying, "Don't you care that we are perishing?" He gets up and tells the waves and the wind to be quiet and still. Truthfully if that were me in the boat, I'd be bragging about what just took place, but Jesus rebuked them for their lack of faith.

They forgot He said they were going to the other side. They did not realize that when Jesus declares something, all the powers of Hell cannot keep it from happening. And they will try. In a manner of speaking, I believe He is also teaching that the boundaries of The Kingdom don't just happen. They expand in the midst of storms and opposition.

NEW DIMENSIONS OF RELATIONSHIP

John 16:16-22 says:

A little while, and you will not see Me; and again a little while, and you will see Me, because I go to the Father. Then some of His disciples said among themselves, 'What is this that He says to us, A little while, and you will not see Me; and again a little while, and you will see Me,' and, 'because I go to the Father?'" They said therefore, What is this that He says, 'A little while'? We do not know what He is saying." Now Jesus knew that they desired to ask Him, and He said to them, "Are you inquiring among yourselves about what I said, 'A little while, and you will not see Me; and again a little while, and you will see Me?' Most assuredly, I say to you that you will weep and lament, but the world will rejoice; and you will be sorrowful, but your sorrow will be turned into joy. A woman, when she is in labor, has sorrow because her hour has come; but as soon as she has given birth to the child, she no longer remembers the anguish, for joy that a human being has been born into the world. Therefore you now have sorrow; but I will see you again and your heart will rejoice, and your joy no one will take from you.

Let's stop here. What He is saying is really a prophetic declaration about the coming suffering, death, burial, resurrection and ascension of Jesus. Some scholars are convinced that the vast majority of this gospel is simply recording the last few weeks of Jesus' life. Unlike the other three gospels which are called synoptic (Matthew, Mark and Luke are written from a similar point of view this is called "synoptic." John's gospel stands alone).

The metaphor he chose here for a woman in labor is a good

one because it helps connect this moment of the "here and now" to the "then and there" or the present with the future.

Further in Luke 8 we read:

And in that day you will ask Me nothing. Most assuredly, I say to you, whatever you ask the Father in My name He will give you. Until now you have asked nothing in My name. Ask, and you will receive, that your joy may be full.

Don't miss this point. At this point they were going to Jesus for all of their needs. Jesus would take them to the Father. Now that all changes. From this moment on they are given the "check book." They have the privilege of interacting directly with the Father. Intimacy with the Father is theirs for the taking.

GETTING PREGNANT

I did a check on infant mortality rates in the world. The statistics are based on a 1,000 births. I was very surprised to see that the United States does not have the lowest rate in the world. We are 178th with 6.26 deaths per 1,000. There are forty five countries with lower death rates. Singapore is the lowest with 2.31. My point is that today husbands and wives usually don't talk about the probability of survival for the children they hope to bring into this world. Few ever really get into the rigors of childbirth as an issue as to whether or not they will have children. One reason is really simple. For the joy set before them, women will endure much pain to hold that baby in their arms.

I think, if women could birth in phases and just do a little at a time, few babies would ever be born The fact is there's no turning back. Once it starts there's no stopping it.

Jesus connects this birth process with prayer. The last two verses point to the subject of prayer. And Jesus reveals the heart of the Father when he clarifies one of the goals as *"you will receive, that your joy may be full."* Remember, they have been with

Him for about three years witnessing the invasion of Heaven on earth by seeing eyes recreated, dead people raised and insane people delivered. His disciples got it right when they concluded it was a move of God that was initiated and sustained because He spent time being with and talking with His Father. We call that prayer. Jesus wants us to be full of something that spills out onto the places where we live and move and have our being. My friend Kevin Dedmon said it this way, "We are supposed to be so filled that we leak."

I have Muslim friends that I pray will one day open their hearts to Jesus, and not just as a prophet (because they do believe that He was a prophet). I pray He would become their Lord and Savior. Most Muslims have an extreme view of God as sovereign. In other words, if you get killed in a car accident, it's God's will. If you get cancer and die, it's God's will. If your daughter gets raped, it's God's will. Everything happens because God willed it to happen. If you have that perspective, what's the point of praying? There are some Christians who think like that as well.

I read some of the prayers Muslims pray throughout the day, and the word that jumped off the pages for me was "beg." They beg Allah for certain things to happen. It's as if his mind is already made up, and if you beg him, maybe just maybe, things will turn out differently. What Jesus introduces to us here is radically different from that.

SOVEREIGNTY AND ROYALTY

John Wesley said, "God does nothing in response to the affairs of men except in response to prayer."[11] This statement alone would bring debates galore between major sects of Christianity. I think Wesley's idea is probably right. However, I would not make a doctrine out of it. Here is what I mean. God is God and can do anything His heart desires. Would you agree with that?

He has chosen to give us free will, even at the risk that some of us will reject Him and choose the other kingdom over His. Another thing He has done is commit Himself to restricting His rule over the earth to include us. In Luke it tells us that a man named Simeon and a prophetess named Anna had been fasting and praying for decades for the Messiah to come. Why pray for something that God is going to do anyway? Great question.

God has created beings like angels to do all sorts of things, way beyond my comprehension, even to the point of assigning them to minister to us. That's pretty amazing. He could give them the responsibility of preaching the gospel, but He has reserved that for us. Why? Because in delegating that thing to us, He is inviting us to share in the glory of His Kingdom. He invites me to have influence in the outcome of the affairs of men even though I don't get it right all of the time.

Add to that mystery the fact that sometimes I pray for years over a matter, and at other times it seems the moment I utter a prayer, the answer comes immediately. The challenge is not to allow the offense of that tension to harden my heart, or to some-how conclude that I must be praying the wrong way.

There is an eternal consequence to prayer that we some-times forget about. Every believer is called to rule and reign with Christ. In our Western mindset, we believe that means we will be the boss. It means wherever you fall in that scheme of King-dom rule, you will be greatest because you have learned to be a servant leader to honor, to bless and to be governed by love. You see, God tethered Himself to a covenant. That covenant gives me both the right and the choice to partner with Him in affecting the affairs of men. I don't have to beg for something He has al-ready committed Himself to.

As a kid, when I heard things in church such as, "It's more blessed to give than to receive," I thought that must have been written by some nutty adult because I could not imagine that to be true. When I became a parent, I finally got it. It's so much greater to give presents to my kids, than to receive them. It's just more fun.

When we pray and trust God for a response to our prayers there is a joy that happens inside of us, that in turn delights the heart of your Dad in Heaven. By the way, I'm glad He negates any prayers that are dumb, because I have prayed a few of them. I am convinced that if God answered every prayer, even by Christians, no team would ever win a football game and we'd never have a president. I'm glad He has veto power over some of the crazy things we pray for.

I wish I had an answer for every question about prayer, but I don't. Can I tell you a little secret? No one does. And if they say they do, smile on your way out the door. This much I do know. The more time I spend with Him, the fewer questions I have. In Hebrews 12:2 it says that He is the author and finisher of our faith. It seems apparent that if you spend more time with the Author He will finish your faith.

WAITING IS NOT PASSIVE

The disciples were told by Jesus to wait in Jerusalem until they received power. The concept of wait doesn't make sense in the way most of us think about it today. Wait wasn't a cozy "Kum Ba Yah" around the bonfire concept. What is meant was that 120 people who took Jesus' command seriously, went and offered "petitions and supplications." As I understand it, petitions are requests you make one time. Have you ever signed a petition for change? You signed it and waited for a response.

Supplication is different. It would be like someone driving to our church service and running out of gas about 100 feet from our parking lot. Pretend the vehicle is one of those big Hummers and one of our men runs out there to push it into the parking lot. A few other guys see that he is barely moving the vehicle, so they join in. Finally the fifth guy shows up, and as they put their shoulders together to heave, the Hummer begins to move and they push it into our lot.

It's that kind of prayer you are praying, to move something much bigger than you can handle on your own. In the Kingdom, waiting implies a militant, pressing-in kind of prayer. One hundred and twenty people prayed together for ten days, even though they did not know what it would look like when the Holy

Spirit came, but nevertheless they knew they were to contend for it. "Waiting" to them was waging spiritual warfare as a group.

When it comes Peter says in Acts 2:16, *"This is that which was prophesied by Joel."* If you go back and look at that prophecy almost none of it literally took place as Joel described on that day. Similarly, there are major movements in the church today that have charts and graphs about all the future holds as it relates to prophecy. I know, because I used to have some of them. I have since realized that the "charts and graphs" mentality is exactly what caused the leaders of Jesus' day to completely reject His arrival. Prophecy is not given so you can neatly compartmentalize your eschatology. It is given to reveal the heart of the Father and to allow the Holy Spirit to sovereignly breathe upon that prophetic word and say, *"This is that which was prophesied."*

The next corporate meeting occurred in Acts 4. In it we see that leaders in the church were arrested because of a miracle performed which led to many conversions. Peter and John were threatened for preaching and performing miracles, and when they regrouped with the "corporate" body they prayed like this,

Acts 4:29-31:

> *Now, Lord, look on their threats, and grant to Your servants that with all boldness they may speak Your word, by stretching out Your hand to heal, and that signs and wonders may be done through the name of Your holy servant Jesus." (Didn't Jesus promise them this would happen before He left? Yes. They are reminding Him of His word.) And when they had prayed, the place where they were assembled together was shaken; and they were all filled with the Holy Spirit, and they spoke the word of God with boldness.*

This is not meditative, contemplative, soaking prayer. Those are important prayers, but this is different because it has urgency to it. It's fervent, it's forceful; like what you hear when you go to see your favorite NFL team play, except with a spiritual twist.

Are you promoting emotionalism? No, but I'm not afraid of it. It's that silent emotionalism that provokes me. Maybe someone told you that you are shy, but you don't have to buy into that. In this scripture, we see people who desperately want to see God increase His Presence in their city, and they prayed so passionately that it shook the building. I often say to our church that I want to be in this building when the house shakes. And I mean it.

We have a number of young mothers in our church, and I know that some of them consider themselves "shy" and yet I can completely debunk this once and for all. Let's take one of those so called shy mothers when she takes her child to the park. She is distracted momentarily, and then picture some man grabbing her child out of the stroller and running away with him or her. You would see a lamb transform instantly into a killer lion that will rip your lips off to protect that child. The only difference is that before she was locked up in herself, and in a moment became desperate and shed all shyness for what was at stake. Beloved, if you really knew what was at stake, you'd shed your shyness and become desperate for God to show up.

Acts 12:5-11 tells how Herod beheaded James because it gave him more support from the Jews. The corporate church gathered to pray to stop the plans of a man who was bent on evil.

Peter was therefore kept in prison, but constant prayer was offered to God for him by the church. And when Herod was about to bring him out, that night Peter was sleeping, bound with two chains between two soldiers; and the guards before the door were keeping the prison. Now behold, an angel of the Lord stood by him, and a light shone in the prison; and he struck Peter on the side and raised him up, saying, "Arise quickly!" And his chains fell off his hands. Then the angel said to him, "Gird yourself and tie on your sandals;" and so he did. And he said to him, "Put on your garment and follow me." So he went out and followed him, and did not know that what was done by the angel was real, but thought he was seeing a vision. When they were past the first and the second guard posts, they came to the iron gate that leads to the city, which opened to them of its own accord; and they went out and went down one street, and immediately the angel departed from him. And when Peter had come to himself, he said, "Now I know for certain that the Lord has sent His angel, and has delivered me from the hand of Herod and from all the expectation of the Jewish people.

What happened? A desperate, corporate prayer happened to release Peter from an unjust death sentence. It released an angel to come like a whirlwind to keep the blood-lust of a hostile crowd and maniacal king from taking Peter's life. So, first we see wind and fire, then we see earthquakes, and now we see angels responding to the corporate prayer of desperate people. You might say I'm not desperate enough to pray like that, so wouldn't it be hypocritical to pray that way? The answer is no. Denying your emotions as an outcrop of obedience is not hypocritical. It's obedience because He gave us the record of what works in this book.

There is something I have seen through the years that has proven time and time again to be an ignition point for corporate prayer. You can be unmotivated by your flesh to pray and intercede in a particular moment, and then someone with fire in their bones prays and it does something inside of you to nudge you to pray. If you're weak in faith and discouraged, don't hang around your depressed friends. Find someone with fire in their soul, and do whatever you can to have it jump on to you.

Is being loud important in corporate prayer meetings? No, but being desperate is essential. Allow yourself to be moved. In the Kingdom, you pray because it's the right thing to do. In the world, you pray because you feel like it. In the Kingdom, you do it regardless, and then the feelings follow. If I only pray fervently when I feel desperate, then I only pray when I have a problem.

It is my personal opinion and experience that if you will pray with fervency, you will avert many crises. Do you remember Jesus' words, "Lead us not into temptation?" The absolute greatest crisis in the Book is when sin begins to look appealing to you. Do you know that applied to Him? At His weakest moment, hours before He was supposed to die, all of Hell was unleashed upon Him. Laying there in the garden...alone...wondering if there is any other way out. Jesus told his twelve disciples to pray so they wouldn't fall into temptation. They slept instead.

There He is alone, bombarded with temptation, and doing hand-to-hand combat with the devil in prayer. And because He was in anguish and agony He prayed more. The greatest heavy weight fight in the universe and Jesus put on the brass knuckles and took it to another level and said essentially, "I'm going to keep swinging until one of us goes down and it ain't going to be me." I remember that scene in *The Passion of the Christ* when Jesus is in the Garden. When He wins that battle of temptation, and finally gets up and stomps on the serpent, I about came out of my seat!

I believe and am deeply convinced of Kingdom reciprocity. I am also convinced that if you will go to battle for another Christian who is struggling with sin, you will find victory when you face the same crisis. At our church we meet on Tuesday mornings for corporate intercession. We have done this for some time now. It is rare that I ever miss. There are many mornings when I am tired and worn out. I go then because if I am willing to give when I don't feel like giving, and pray when I don't feel like praying, I believe God will remember those mornings and pull me out of temptations that could take me out!

Finally, the issue of agreement is huge in the Kingdom. Matthew 18:18-20 says:

Again I say to you that if two of you agree on earth concerning anything that they ask, it will be done for them by My Father in heaven. For where two or three are gathered together in My name, I am there in the midst of them.

The context is discipline within the church, but the overarching application is corporate.

Ecclesiastes 4:12 says:

…a threefold cord is not easily broken.

This is best explained with fishing line. If I had a camera I could show you a piece of monofilament fishing line that was fifty pound test. "Mono" means one strand. In recent years, they have come up with something called braided fishing line. They are very thin multiple layers of fabric and the diameter of braided fishing line is only about half of the mono at fifty pound test. The principle is that when you use multiple strands of the same strength, instead of addition there is multiplication. In other words if you take five strands of ten pound test and braid them together, it will produce something like eighty pound test.

This is why the Bible says that *"one will chase a thousand and two ten thousand."* This is the strength of corporate prayer meetings. King David tapped into this.

In 1 Kings 8:16-17 one of the greatest events in all of human history is recorded. It was the building of the Temple in Jerusalem.

Since the day that I brought My people Israel out of Egypt, I have chosen no city from any tribe of Israel in which to build a house, that My name might be there; but I chose David to be over My people Israel.' Now it was in the heart of my father David to build a temple for the name of the Lord God of Israel.

The Lord chooses men. He then blesses what's in their heart as an answer to prayer. God bought into David's vision so much so that when Jesus arrives in the temple one day He braids some cord together like a whip and drives out the corrupt merchants.

He says, *"My house shall be called a house of prayer."* The heart of David was to have a place where corporate prayer would ascend to God day and night. In Acts 15 James says that God's promise is to rebuild the Tabernacle of David, not the Temple of Solomon. It is a prophetic call echoing down to us today that God wants the Church not to neglect corporate gatherings to intercede for our lands. In doing that He partners with us for what's on our hearts as well. Isn't that simply amazing?

THE POWER OF "ONE"

2 Corinthians 8:9 says:

You know the generous grace of our Lord Jesus Christ. Though He was rich, yet for your sakes He became poor, so that by His poverty He could make you rich.

I want to open this chapter by asking if you really believe that? Most of you would say yes, but you would catapult that into the millennium or Heaven. Unfortunately, Paul doesn't give us that kind of wiggle room. Many of us think that in our current state of existence we are not worthy to have such riches.

In Proverbs 30:21-22 it says:

There are three things that make the earth tremble—no, four it cannot endure: a pauper who becomes a king...

Kris Vallotton has done a masterful work in demonstrating the principle of supernatural royalty in his book, The Supernatural Ways of Royalty. The reality is that though we are called royal by our Creator, we often operate and live out our lives as paupers. In doing that we destroy the very thing God has called us and empowered us to do. Again, I am not promoting a false sense of worth, or arrogance, or prideful attitudes about ourselves.

Someone said we are supposed to be great commission people with a great commandment heart.[12] That means we cannot fulfill our portion of the great commission in a manner pleasing to the Father unless we have a heart that first loves Him, and second loves our neighbor as we love Him. Actually, it doesn't say that. It says to love our neighbor as ourselves. You can't do that if you don't love yourself in the manner He values us.

There are some who would accuse me of promoting carnality and prideful arrogance with statements like this. Let me see if I can illustrate this better. Let's pretend that you painted an amazing portrait that was hanging in the lobby of a church. One day after services I come along with some friends and start talking about the painting and I have no clue you painted it.

I say, "That is a weird painting. I wouldn't put that picture in my bathroom, much less in the lobby of a church." Now as the artist hearing me criticize your work, how does that make you feel?

God says that I am made in the image and likeness of Him. I am His handiwork. I am royalty, His treasure. How do you think the One who created me feels if I start running you down and calling you a worm, a nobody, a mere piece of fallen flesh? He did not redeem me to toss me on a heap of trash.

DISCOVERING THE POSER

Some years ago I was involved in mentoring a pastor and a group of his leaders. One day this pastor gave me a check for a large sum of money. I went home and showed my wife, and she too was stunned. All of a sudden I started noticing that I wasn't looking forward to being with these people as much as before I received that love gift. Why?

Because deep in my heart I really didn't think I was worth that kind of blessing. Before I knew it, I was thinking that if they really got to know me they might think the money they gave me was not a good idea. In other words, I was not worth it. The pauper in me wanted to say, "Gee I can't accept that money because I'm really not worth that much." The poser in me looked for ways to avoid growing in deeper intimacy with them by avoiding opportunities to spend time with them.

That's what I call thinking like a pauper and acting like a poser. Because the very thing that was brought to me I was trying to run from. A prince doesn't think like that.

I was reading parts of a book called *Tipping Points* by Malcolm Gladwell. It's not a Christian book, and some of the case studies are not for the faint of heart, but something important is brought to the surface in this book. I believe that even though he doesn't say it this way Gladwell is saying that paupers gather in large crowds and feel good about each other in those settings, but a prince/princess can create tipping points in their culture. Early in the book he talks about a scene that took place in 1964 that I actually remembered hearing about when living in upstate New York.

This situation happened in New York City when a woman was chased down, robbed and brutally murdered while 38 people watched and did nothing. This was over a period of more than 30 minutes. The amazing part of the story is that not one of them called the police. Over time, sociologists have done studies of crimes like this where more than one person witnessed a crime similar to this. They said that if one person witnesses a crime, they most likely will call the police. If three people witness it, the number drops significantly. The conclusion was that the larger the crowd, the less likely anyone would be to call the police while witnessing a heinous act.

One of the conclusions of this author is that crowds do not create tipping points - individuals create tipping points. That strikes a chord in me because that sounds like the Bible. As Americans we think that if we can gather enough people for a specific cause we can change our culture. Before I make this statement please listen to me carefully. I am not opposed to large prayer gatherings and national prayer movements. Nor am I suggesting they don't influence the spiritual atmosphere of our nation. But in many Christians' minds we think that God looks down and says, "Hmm…one million people in the mall of Washington

DC…I'll do something powerful." But if only 50,000 show…well maybe He's not so impressed. But the Bible says things like, "I am searching the earth looking for a man who I can show myself mighty through." In Isaiah 6, God asks the question, "Who will go for us?" Isaiah doesn't say, "We will," he says, "I will." God uses him as a tipping point in his nation.

Joseph was a prince in Egypt. He was a tipping point for the people of God. Moses, Nehemiah, and many others were as well. When a person begins to think with a royal mindset, they don't look to the strength of the crowd, they look to the strength of the King over them. History has demonstrated that over and over again. What they discovered in that tragedy in New York City is that the crowd of 38 people thought "someone else" called the police. It becomes easy to be impressed with the large size of the group, and you don't feel personally responsible to act.

We see that here in the Children's ministry at church. As they come to services, people will look in the nursery or classroom and see groups of children and several adults serving, and when it's time for them to serve on a Sunday morning, if something comes up, they not only don't show for the service, I am told many don't even call. They think someone else will cover. See how this can seep down into our lives?

Read the life of Daniel and it becomes clear that Nebuchadnezzar, King of Babylon, thinks he has captured four Hebrew boys, but before the story ends it's as if those four boys captured Babylon. Israel couldn't defeat Babylon with its army, instead God took four teenagers and rocked that kingdom from the inside out. Daniel acted like a prince, not a pauper. Eventually Babylon fell to the Medo-Persian Empire. A brand new world power emerges, and Cyrus discovers Daniel because of prophetic declarations and dream interpretations. These four boys continue to be tipping points until one day Cyrus releases the Jews to go back and rebuild a temple and even finances the project from his own treasury.

In Jeremiah 5:1:

Run to and fro through the streets of Jerusalem; see now and know; And seek in her open places if you can find a man, if there is anyone who executes judgment, who seeks the truth, and I will pardon her.

Did you get that? He didn't say, "See if you can gather a crowd." He said, "Find me a person, someone who realizes that I am King, and as my royal offspring, I will do amazing things. Find me someone who knows who I am, and who they are, and I will release things in their life. These things don't happen because of a crowd.

When I was three years old, in December of 1955, there was a woman in Montgomery, Alabama who for all of her 42 years would get on a bus and have a seat assignment. You see, she was a black woman, and in those days all black people were expected to sit in the back. One day, something inside of her would not allow her to follow the crowd. In my opinion, Rosa Parks had a revelation of who she was in the sight of God. She was not a pauper, she was a princess, and princesses don't sit in the back of the bus. They sit wherever they want. The driver of the bus told her to sit in the back, or he would call the police. Rosa would not move and became a tipping point for that time.

Shortly after that, there was another Martin Luther that came along. Except this one had the last name of King. I find it fascinating that 431 years before Martin Luther King Jr. was born, the first Martin Luther stood up under religious tyranny and said enough is enough. There is a priesthood of believers, and all believers are a royal priesthood. We are not paupers, but King's kids.

Martin Luther King Jr. said enough is enough. When most thought that change could only come with bloodshed, he refused to endorse any form of violence. The "crowd" said let's riot, let's burn and overthrow. He refused. I believe in his heart he knew he was not a pauper, but a prince because that's what God called him.

One day, King was sitting in his house and some men from the Ku Klux Klan pulled up to his house and ignited a bomb that blew up the front of his home. For some reason, the explosion stopped just short of his wife and daughter. Out from the rubble came King and his family, and many black people said, "The only way this is ever going to change is through violent revolution." They wanted him to go out in front of his destroyed home and preach a violent uprising. He refused. Instead, he stood outside and forgave his enemies.

One very wealthy business man came forward and offered him a million dollars to build the church of his dreams if he would only stop this movement. He refused. You see Martin Luther King Jr. knew another King. His name is Jesus of Nazareth, King of kings, and because his daddy was King, he was going to follow that example. That's what princes do. They act like royalty.

Genesis 1:28 makes it clear that we were born to rule:

Then God blessed them, and God said to them, "Be fruitful and multiply; fill the earth and subdue it; have dominion over the fish of the sea, over the birds of the air, and over every living thing that moves on the earth."

Genesis 3:22-23 says we were banished from the Kingdom:

Then the LORD God said, "Behold, the man has become like one of Us, to know good and evil. And now, lest he put out his hand and take also of the tree of life, and eat, and live forever"— therefore the LORD God sent him out of the garden of Eden to till the ground from which he was taken.

Why did this happen? Because Adam believed a lie and empowered the liar. God in His mercy was about to begin to reverse that curse and one day restore paradise lost.

ON EARTH AS IT IS IN HEAVEN

I began this book by questioning the validity of one of the most common reasons for intercession in the corporate church today.

It is in 2 Chronicles 7:14:

If My people who are called by My name will humble them-selves, and pray and seek My face, and turn from their wicked ways, then I will hear from heaven, and will forgive their sin and heal their land.

The challenge arises in the verse preceding this verse: *"When I shut up heaven and there is no rain, or command the locusts to devour the land, or send pestilence among My people"* (v.13). What is directly implied here is that if God sees fit, He will send judgment upon His people, and when that happens, the prescription for this judgment is in verse 14. If this is true then we have a great contradiction in the life, mission and ministry of Jesus of Nazareth. Remember in Luke 16:16, Jesus said, *"The Law and the prophets were until John, but now that Kingdom of God has come and many are pressing into it."* It is His clearest statement of transition in the gospels. This epic transition is now in place until His return to "judge the living and the dead."

UNPUNISHABLE

Danny Silk published a book some time ago entitled *Culture of Honor*. It is one of the books I keep on hand in my private library. Danny has named one of the sections in the book "Unpunishable". In it he states, "He (Jesus) has made each and every one of us unpunishable." What Danny meant by this is that under the Old Covenant there was no question of reprisal from God for sin. The Law demanded it.

Within the Law were a plethora of rules required to keep our relationship with God in "order." This began the day the children of Israel told Moses they did not want to go to the mountain of God, but that he should go to God and tell them what the "rules" were. That day marked the beginning of man's relationship with God being based on his relationship with rules. The "barometer" for how well you were doing in the sight of God would be determined by how well you kept the rules.

It also set the tone for who Israel was allowed to have meaningful relationship with. They were forbidden to have fellowship with pagans and were at times even commanded to exterminate them for fear of contamination of their people. Then came the cross. It changed everything, in every way. It obliterated the lines of separation between us and our Creator; and between Christians and the world.

In 1 John 4:16-19 it says:

"God is love, and all who live in love live in God, and God lives in them. And as we live in God, our love grows more perfect. So we will not be afraid on the day of judgment, but we can face Him with confidence because we live like Jesus here in this world. Such love has no fear, because perfect love expels all fear. If we are afraid, it is for fear of punishment, and this shows that we have not fully experienced his perfect love. We love each other because he loved us first. (NLT)

Here is how this plays out in our lives. If we choose to have a relationship with God by having relationship with His rules, we have placed ourselves "under" the law. We are subject to punishment when we fail. On the other hand, those who choose to have a relationship with God based upon the "love of God in Christ Jesus" are subject to grace when they stumble. To state it in simple terms, under the law punishment is due. However, in Christ there is grace. In addition, within this relationship comes the opportunity to be in fellowship with sinners who need to know the

God of this stunning love relationship.

Let's return back to 2 Chronicles 7:14 which says:

If My people who are called by My name will humble them-selves, and pray and seek My face, and turn from their wicked ways, then I will hear from heaven, and will forgive their sin and heal their land.

What are those "wicked ways?"

In verse 17 it says:

As for you, if you walk before Me as your father David walked, and do according to all that I have commanded you, and if you keep My statutes and My judgments...

There you have it. The restoration of favor with God and the thwarting of judgments against them were based upon their obeying God's laws and statutes. Their relationship with God was predicated upon their relationship with His rules. The question then begs to be asked, is this 2 Chronicles section a valid premise from which Christians should intercede for the Church, or even the world around us? Think it through.

If God was in Christ reconciling the world to Himself by not counting their transgressions against them, why would we then pray as though He still is? If The Father gave all judgment to The Son and The Son stated clearly that He did not come to judge the world but to save it, then why would we pray as if He is judging it?

The oft quoted saying, "If God does not judge America for her sins of_____ (you fill in the blanks), then He owes Sodom and Gomorrah an apology" then becomes an illegal demand upon the mercy of God. In fact may I pose this question? Could it even be an affront to His promises?

Chapter 6 | OUR AUTHORITY

Our Metron

In 2 Corinthians 10:15-16, Paul uses a Greek word "metron" to describe an area of influence or authority that is assigned to him as the apostolic leader of the church located in that city. He basically says, he has been given this metron by God to exercise Kingdom authority over that region. In contrast, Paul acknowledges that in other places he does not have the right to exercise this authority, because it was given to someone else. When my wife Lisa and I answered the call to lead Harvest in1996, we bought land and committed ourselves to the people of this land, and this became our "metron." So if I am not being faithful in the "metron" He has assigned to me, I have no business going other places to minister unless He has sent me there.

Within this metron God has some very important things to say in this regard. In Jeremiah 29 we see King Nebuchadnezzar capture the city of Jerusalem and take many of the people back to Babylon. There were "so called" Israelite prophets rising up saying, "We're not going to be here long. Soon the Lord will come and take us back." It reminds me of the beginning of the book of Acts when the disciples watched Jesus ascend to Heaven and the angel said, "What are you doing gazing into the sky? He's not here." In other words, He did what He said He would do; now you go and do what He told you to do.

Jeremiah has a "good news/bad news" contrast. The good news is that God is going to bless and prosper you. The bad news is that He is going to do that while you are captives in Babylon. Similar to today, He wants to bless us here and now, within the captivity all of us as believers share in this world that is fallen, decaying and cursed.

The challenge I see is that we have many people in the church who are so focused on His return that they are not fulfilling their Kingdom responsibilities now. They have lots of charts, books and folks using their daily newspapers alongside their Bibles to determine where we are on someone's eschatological chart. The focus becomes "the end of the world is near" instead of "the Kingdom of God is at hand." It removes from us the responsibility of contending for "on earth as it is in heaven." It removes from us the responsibility of seeing lives change, homes change, churches change, and cities change. I had all the charts and all the books, and it dawned on me that Jesus didn't make it clear to us when He will be returning for a reason. He didn't want us to know ☺.

All you need to do is go back and see what Jesus said to His disciples in Acts 1. They were doing the same thing. He said, "It's not for you to know the times and seasons." Somehow we have acquired some sense of arrogance about this that says, "Well He didn't want them to know, but it's OK for us to try and figure it out." We have the same job they had.

Jeremiah 29:4-14 says:

Thus says the Lord of hosts, the God of Israel, to all who were carried away captive, whom I have caused to be carried away from Jerusalem to Babylon: "Build houses and dwell in them; plant gardens and eat their fruit. Take wives and beget sons and daughters; and take wives for your sons and give your daughters to husbands, so that they may bear sons and daughters—that you may be increased there, and not diminished. And seek the peace of the city where I have caused you to be carried away captive, and pray to the Lord for it; for in its peace you will have peace."

For thus says the Lord of hosts, the God of Israel: "Do not let your prophets and your diviners who are in your midst deceive you, nor listen to your dreams which you cause to be dreamed. For they prophesy falsely to you in My name; I have not sent them, says the Lord. For thus says the Lord: After seventy years are completed at Babylon, I will visit you and perform My good word toward you, and cause you to return to this place. For I know the thoughts that I think toward you, says the Lord, thoughts of peace and not of evil, to give you a future and a hope. Then you will call upon Me and go and pray to Me, and I will listen to you. And you will seek Me and find Me, when you search for Me with all your heart. I will be found by you, says the Lord, and I will bring you back from your captivity.

PEACE

Here is what I see God attempting to get across to His people. He is trying to move them from being a need-oriented people, focused on their prosperity, to having a vision of prosperity for the region where they live. In other words, they prefer others over themselves, and in doing this find something supernatural occurring there. The laws of the Kingdom are by and large the opposite of what we had before we became believers. (Up is down....to gain life you must die....to get you must give...the least becomes the greatest.) It says to me that His world is right side up and everything else is upside down.

In Jeremiah 29:7 it says:

And seek the peace of the city where I have caused you to be carried away captive, and pray to the Lord for it; for in its peace you will have peace..

There is a very common word used here that most people have heard. It's the Hebrew word "shalom." This word can be translated various ways. Sometimes it means tranquility, rest and a calmness that comes when life is good. It can mean the absence of war and stability in a nation. It can mean that you have good health. It can mean literal prosperity.

Psalm 73:3 says:

For I was envious at the foolish, when I saw the prosperity of the wicked.

The word translated "prosperity" is the word shalom.

At my daughter Emma's going away party for a mission trip, one of her classmates called me a hippie. Emma laughed and agreed that this was so during my college days. I recall that during that time peace meant that we would stop the war in Vietnam and do away with the armed forces draft, along with nuclear disarmament. I think we even invented the original peace sign. The Bible has a different take on the word. Peace is not the absence of war. It is the presence of God—the Prince of Peace.

It covers every dimension of our being - spirit, soul and body. Peace is not passive. It is powerful and assertive. When Jesus faced the raging storm on the Sea of Galilee what did He say? *"Peace...be still"* (Mark 4:39). He commanded peace to overtake chaos. When Jesus healed the woman with the issue of blood in Luke 8:48 He said, *"Go in peace...your faith has made you whole."*

Jeremiah 29:7 says:

And seek the peace of the city where I have caused you to be carried away captive, and pray to the Lord for it; for in its peace you will have peace.

Let me personalize this for you. Seek the health, welfare, prosperity, tranquility, healing and wholeness of the place where you live, as I do for Hampton Roads. Go after it aggressively, wholeheartedly and passionately. Why? Because in this place is your peace. Don't be looking to the sky. Don't live with your bags packed. Don't look for an out. Plant, harvest, marry and multiply. Sounds like a multi-generational vision to me.

First, we need to make some adjustments in the way we approach the "last days." Some have written off this world and when something bad or catastrophic happens, we affirm it as something good. "Things are only going to get worse" is often the Christian mantra of this country.

The Bible says we are to hasten the return of the Lord. What that looks like to me, according to the book of Revelation is that the *"bride has made herself ready."* How? She makes Herself by sharing intimacy with God and by carrying out his or her responsibilities to release the gospel of The Kingdom around the world.

The second thing I pray would be reformed in the church is our view of the world around us. We are in the world, but not of the world. What does that mean? It means that when we carry the Kingdom, it is supposed to bring some of Heaven to this planet. It's not a retreat mentality; it's an over-comer mentality and a blessing mentality.

Psalm 67:5-7 says:

May the nations praise you, O God. Yes, may all the nations praise you. Then the earth will yield its harvests, and God, our God, will richly bless us Yes, God will bless us, and people all over the world will fear him.

As I see it, plan "A" is to bring blessing and bounty to us so that the world will know who He is. We have been given a commission from The Lord that cannot be accomplished with human ingenuity alone. It requires supernatural provision. Plan "B" is through trial, pain and conflict. How is it that famous musicians can make such amazing music that is sounds like the instruments can talk. Yet they don't know God? How is it that an architect who doesn't know God can create stunning buildings that leave you awestruck?

The devil didn't inspire them; he can't create anything. He can only distort and counterfeit. The gift in them came from the Creator. We can honor Him by honoring the gift in them. Let's talk about the "boycott mentality" and think about how that squares with what God told Jeremiah to do. Do you think there just might have been some ungodliness in that culture? There were things that went on in Babylon that would make Las Vegas look tame. God didn't say to protest, He said to pray for prosperity. It's time for the church not to be known for what it doesn't do.

I have yet to meet an unbeliever who was led to Jesus because I don't drink or smoke.

To bring it home, here is what I would like to propose. Pick a business in your area and contact the manager or owner. Tell them you are going to pray for the prosperity of the business, and even ask them for specific things to pray for. Then ask if you may contact them once or twice a year see how the business is doing.

Or, if you're in business as an owner or major partner, find a similar business in the area and ask the owner if it would be okay for you to pray for the prosperity of the business. In effect, you are praying for your competition. This is an amazing act. Talk about a powerful impact. In fact, tell them that you may occasionally come on the property to pray, but that you will not do it conspicuously.

Why? Because we are not here on this planet to make the great escape. We are here to make a powerful, positive impact in our city. We pray for miracles each week at our church for physical healings. Similarly, do you think God will heal someone's business? Imagine the impact if you became the vessel of His deliverance for a business that was going downhill, and God turned it around.

In Jeremiah 29: 7 it says, *"And seek the peace of the city where I have caused you to be carried away captive, and pray to the Lord for it; for in its peace you will have peace."* Does that sound like God wants to judge your city? More importantly has He changed His mind?[13]

HOPE

Romans 8:22-25 says:

For we know that the whole creation groans and labors with birth pangs together until now. Not only that, but we also who have the first fruits of the Spirit, even we ourselves groan within ourselves, eagerly waiting for the adoption, the redemption of our body. For we were saved in this hope, but hope that is seen is not hope; for why does one still hope for what he sees? But if we hope for what we do not see, we eagerly wait for it with perseverance.

Hope is not wishful thinking. It's not something that we take to Las Vegas as we hope to hit it big with the slot machines or at the black jack table.

Paul said later in the same letter 15:13:

Now may the God of (all) hope fill you with all joy and peace in believing, that you may abound in hope by the power of the Holy Spirit.

Paul uses the word *hope* fifteen times in this one letter. Any hope that does not originate from God is false hope. It's wishful thinking. He is the God of all hope. All other is false hope.

Satan, on the other hand, has absolutely no hope to offer. Hope comes from the Kingdom of Heaven; hopelessness comes from the bowels of Hell. In Dante's Inferno (a Middle Ages allegory about a man passing through the gates of Hell) the inscription over the inferno's entrance reads, "Abandon all hope, ye who enter here."

Kingdom hope is defined as the joyful anticipation of good things to come. It is the kind of anticipation that children have on Christmas morning when they are waiting for mom and dad to awaken so they can run downstairs to open their presents. That's Kingdom hope. Hebrews 11 says that it is the substance of faith.

Psalm 139:15-16 says:

My frame was not hidden from You, when I was made in secret, and skillfully wrought in the lowest parts of the earth. Your eyes saw my substance, being yet unformed. And in Your book they all were written, the days fashioned for me, when as yet there were none of them.

God knew us when we were in the early stages of our formation in the womb of our mother. Have you seen images of the baby during the early stages of pregnancy? You were once only "substance" or a mass of complex looking cells that required a microscope to see. With the naked eye you could not see anything. Even though you could not see them, they were the substance of what you became. This is what hope looks like.

We are praying for an awakening in our region. What would happen if hope began to permeate every facet of the region we refer to as home? I believe mental institutions would have a shortage of patients. I believe abortion clinics would close up for lack of business. I believe prostitutes would stop walking the streets of our cities. Hope is a powerful weapon in the hands of God's people. Hope is designed to give life to our spirits, as much as your lungs were designed by God to give oxygen to your body.

We should be a people who inhale the challenges of life and exhale hope. You were made for this. You were created for this. You were designed for this. You see, you are supposed to be a hope vendor, like a soft drink vending machine. Some of us have secretly disqualified ourselves from this role because we have had such a difficult life, or season of life, and we think we are not in any position to give anyone hope. In fact, those who have been through the most have the greatest hope to give. I hope to be able to demonstrate that to you.

Hosea 2:14-15 says:

Therefore, behold, I will allure her, will bring her into the wilderness, and speak comfort to her. I will give her vineyards from there, and the Valley of Achor as a door of hope; she shall sing there, as in the days of her youth, as in the day when she came up from the land of Egypt. And it shall be, in that day," says the Lord...

God uses Hosea's life as a living illustration of the spiritual condition of Israel. He tells Hosea to marry a harlot and to have children with her. It's in the wilderness that hope arises. He will often draw us out into the wilderness to awaken hope in us. It comes alive there. It's found in the dryness and the barrenness. It's found when there seems to be little shelter from the scorching heat. Hope is not an event or a circumstance. It is a mindset.

Hosea 2: 16 adds:

...and it shall be, in that day," says the Lord, "That you will call Me 'My Husband,' and no longer call Me 'My Master,' for I will take from her mouth the names of the Baals, and they shall be remembered by their name no more. In that day I will make a covenant for them with the beasts of the field, with the birds of the air.

What is God doing? He's prophesying hope in a nation of people who have rejected Him and are soon going to go into captivity.

In 1 Corinthians 13:13 Paul qualifies the three greatest virtues of life: faith, hope and love. The greatest is love. But what was he saying about the other two? "The greatest" means that love will exist in all of eternity. Faith and hope are tethered to this earth and this age. Neither is necessary in Heaven.

Have you ever heard of a woman called Sojourner Truth? If you're a woman, you need to teach your children about this American hero. She was a woman in the 1800s which was strike number one against her. Strike number two was that she was born into slavery. She was like a black William Wilberforce. She was a candidate for hopelessness. Her husband was beaten to death because her owner didn't want her to have babies from a man he did not own. Her children were all sold into slavery like cattle at an auction. She lived to the age of eighty-six and had every reason to give up on life. Never taught to read or write, she had a personal encounter with the Lord and began learning through others what the Bible says about life. During the visitation from the Lord He called her to become an advocate for the abolition of slavery and women's rights.

This woman was so powerful that when she went to meetings ministers tried to prevent her from speaking. Think about that ☺. Men were afraid of a black woman and former slave. It tells you something about what she carried.

During a conference many spoke of man's superiority over women, their superior intellect, about the manhood of Christ, and even about the sin of our first mother. Suddenly in a moment of boldness, Sojourner Truth stood up and began to make her way to the podium, as a handful of women said things like, "For God's sake, don't let that woman speak, because she'll make this a slavery issue."

Nevertheless, she walked to the podium, took off her sun bonnet and her six-foot frame towered over her audience. An excerpt of her speech from "Ain't I A Woman," shows her bravery and determination. She said,

> Well, children, where there is so much racket there must be something out of kilter. I think that 'twixt the Negroes of the South and the women at the North, all talking about rights, the white men will be in a fix pretty soon. But what's all this here talking about? That man over there says that women need to be helped into carriages, and lifted over ditches, and to have the best place everywhere. Nobody ever helps me into carriages, or over mud-puddles, or gives me any best place! And ain't I a woman? Look at me! Look at my arm! (She flexed her muscles) I have plowed and planted, and gathered into barns, and no man could head me! And ain't I a woman? I could work as much and eat as much as a man - when I could get it - and bear the lash as well! And ain't I a woman? I have borne thirteen children, and seen most all sold off to slavery, and when I cried out with my mother's grief, none but Jesus heard me! And ain't I a wom-

an? Then they talk about this thing in the head; what's this they call it? [member of audience whispers, "intellect"] That's it, honey. What's that got to do with women's rights or Negroes' rights? If my cup won't hold but a pint, and yours holds a quart, wouldn't you be mean not to let me have my little half measure full? Then that little man in black there, he says women can't have as much rights as men, 'cause Christ wasn't a woman! Where did your Christ come from? Where did your Christ come from? From God and a woman! Man had nothing to do with Him. If the first woman God ever made was strong enough to turn the world upside down all alone, these women together ought to be able to turn it back, and get it right side up again! And now they is asking to do it, the men better let them. "Obliged to you for hearing me, and now old Sojourner ain't got nothing more to say.[14]

She became a messenger of Hope. No matter what, she inhaled the circumstances of life and exhaled hope.

2 Corinthians 3:12:

Therefore, since we have such hope, we use great boldness of speech.

This is where she got her boldness. She'd lost her husband and child after child. She faced numerous setbacks and never gave up hope. When she met Jesus, her life became a challenge. He put fire in her bones. No politician can do that. No man can do that. Our political system has become a vendor of false hope. President after president is portrayed as the hope for America. I don't care what political party you support. Your hope is not that party! Christ in you is your hope of glory.

My question today is how many Sojourner Truths are there? These people will not allow the pain and tragedies of their lives to prevent them from being vendors of hope. Don't let anyone disqualify you from that privilege, and it is a privilege. Hope tethers us to Heaven. You become like Jacob's ladder - messengers of Heaven ascending and descending in the world your life. We are connected to the God of all hope.

1 Peter 1:3 says:

Blessed be the God and Father of our Lord Jesus Christ, who according to His great mercy has caused us to be born again to a living hope.

It's our assignment. It's not an event. It's not a circumstance. Sojourner Truth got hold of a hope that made her fearless. Hope caused highly educated men of power to become afraid of a six-foot, ex-slave who couldn't read the headlines on a newspaper. Hope gave her the status of a hero. At least, in my eyes she is. Hope has the ability to influence every sphere you walk in. If you can lay hold of hope like that, you can be a Sojourner Truth yourself.

Her hope was not in a political system or party. Heaven's hope made her fearless in the face of odds few of us will ever face."

Don't let the enemy of your soul steal hope from you. Hope in the hands of a broken person is dangerous. Dangerous to the enemy because it's the one thing that turned a powerless slave girl into one of the mightiest women that ever graced this land called America.

Job 5:16 says:

So the helpless has hope, and unrighteousness must shut its mouth.

When the helpless find hope everything changes. Unrighteousness is the womb of hopelessness.

Proverbs 11:10:

When it goes well with the righteous, the city rejoices...

What would happen to our cities if hope happened? What would happen in our city if hope awakened? What would happen if we cried out for restoration of hope?

In Matthew 6:9-13 it says:

In this manner, therefore, pray: Our Father in heaven, Hallowed be Your name. Your kingdom come. Your will be done on earth as it is in heaven. Give us this day our daily bread. 12 and forgive us our debts, as we forgive our debtors. And do not lead us into temptation, but deliver us from the evil one. For Yours is the kingdom and the power and the glory forever.

Allow me to take a rabbit trail for a moment to help strengthen an important realm of praying and interceding. The Bible says that Jesus preached to multitudes, but spent most of His three year ministry with twelve men. He called them apostles. I have done a fair amount of reading on the subject, and though I am not an expert I have read works by others who are. The word apostle was used by the Greeks long before Jesus was born. They were religious men of renown who represented one of the many Greek gods. They were the literal embodiment of the god they represented, and if you wanted to know anything about that god, you would approach them with your inquiry.

When Rome conquered the Middle East, they borrowed the term and integrated it into their military hierarchy. Roman Apostles were special generals in the Roman army that were sent out to a conquered region to not only retain military order, but more importantly to transform the indigenous population into a true Roman culture. Actually they were often associated with naval or mariner fleets, much like our navy today. "A group of men sent out for one particular purpose not merely to an army but to a band of colonists and their settlement."[15]

Their primary goals were to bring Rome with them including Roman government, culture, values, religion, customs, educational system, language, etc. Their passion was "seek first the kingdom of Rome." Does that sound familiar? They would draw on the literal resources of Rome to transform that region into a micro-Rome.

Over time, people growing up under those kinds of apostolic cities would have a present day reality of the kingdom of Rome, yet many would never realize the fullness of it until they actually went to Rome. "Literal" Rome came fully equipped to assist them. This is a parallel to us as Christians.

I think Jesus meant that when we seek the Kingdom first it comes to us fully equipped. So if you seek to bring the Kingdom to your business, it begins to change it.

Colossians 3:1-2 says:

If then you were raised with Christ, seek those things which are above, where Christ is, sitting at the right hand of God. Set your mind on things above, not on things on the earth.

CHAPTER 7 | DISCIPLINE OR PUNISHMENT?

WHAT ABOUT US?

So what about us? Let's talk about God's discipline for believers.

1 Corinthians 11:31-32 says:

For if we would judge ourselves, we would not be judged. But when we are judged, we are chastened by the Lord, that we may not be condemned with the world.

1 Peter 4:14-17 adds:

So be happy when you are insulted for being a Christian, for then the glorious Spirit of God rests upon you. If you suffer, however, it must not be for murder, stealing, making trouble, or prying into other people's affairs. But it is no shame to suffer for being a Christian. Praise God for the privilege of being called by his name! For the time has come for judgment, and it must begin with God's household. And if judgment begins with us, what terrible fate awaits those who have never obeyed God's Good News? (NLT)

The matter of "judgment" verses "grace" are two truths held in tension with each other in the New Testament. Allow me to use a simple example in my own life to attempt to make this point. In my early days of bow hunting I used a wooden re-curve bow. Each day when the hunt was over I had to leverage the bow between my legs and bend it forward slightly to "unstring" the bow. The reason for this is simple. If you left the bow strung for long periods of time, it would eventually weaken and break when pulling the string back to shoot an arrow. The goal is to preserve the tension in the bow so that it can be used to propel an arrow at lethal speeds through the air into the quarry.

There are a number of truths in scripture that are held in tension like this. One appears to be in conflict with another. Yet like a real bow, without the tension, the arrow doesn't fly. Remember this important truth as you personally process the issues I brought forth in this book. Under this epoch season of grace, this same tension comes into play if language and context are not properly factored into our application of grace and judgment.

First of all, the word judgment comes from the Greek word "krino." It is a decision made by an individual or a group, such as a jury. They make their judgment after hearing all of the evidence presented to them.

In each of these texts (1 Corinthians 11:31-32; 1 Peter 4: 14-17) the central issue of judgment are really directed to individuals as opposed to cities, and nations. Both Paul and Peter are warning the individual members of the church that we need to be very mindful of our own individual spiritual conditions (Romans 9:13; Hebrews 11:20; Hebrews 12:16). Neglecting our birthright and exchanging it for foolish, temporal or sinful things brings discipline from our Father. We need to be vigilant to tend to our souls. That being said, when neglected, we open our lives up to what I call "God's plan B."

Here is the most important distinction held in tension with the concept of discipline. The ultimate goal of discipline should never be punishment.

Hebrews 12:5-8:

And have you forgotten the encouraging words God spoke to you as his children? He said, 'My child, don't make light of the LORD's discipline, and don't give up when He corrects you. For the LORD disciplines those He loves, and he punishes each one he accepts as His child.' As you endure this divine discipline, remember that God is treating you as His own children. Who ever heard of a child who is never disciplined by its father? If God doesn't discipline you as He does all of His children, it means that you are illegitimate and are not really His children at all. (NLT)

The writer of Hebrews is telling us that our very identity as sons of God hinges on the fact that God disciplines us to break off bad habits and bad behavior, to teach us how to be what we are called to be...sons.

Hebrews 5:8-9 states:

Though He was a Son, yet He learned obedience by the things which He suffered. And having been perfected, He became the author of eternal salvation to all who obey Him.

In the first Corinthian letter, Paul is disturbed that they are turning the celebration of the Lord's Table into a worldly party. People are being selfish in the sharing of the meal; others are getting drunk on the celebratory wine and others are demeaning those of meager means. It was not a very honoring atmosphere for the Holy Spirit to operate. Much like with Ananias and Sapphira (Acts 5:1-11), I believe the Holy Spirit responded with severe discipline.

I Corinthians 11:29-32 says:

For he who eats and drinks in an unworthy manner eats and drinks judgment to himself, not discerning the Lord's body. For this reason many are weak and sick among you, and many sleep. For if we would judge ourselves, we would not be judged. But when we are judged, we are chastened by the Lord, that we may not be condemned with the world.

The ultimate form of discipline was a shortened life. Some people died because they refused to judge themselves and therefore the Lord took them home. What was the goal? Not punishment, but redemption. On a personal note, I don't believe Ananias and Sapphira were condemned to Hell as a consequence of lying. In fact, as I think it through, it would be fair to assume that Peter was not expecting that kind of judgment to fall either. After all, who was one of the greatest liars in the New Testament up to that point? None other than Peter, who lied three times on the night Jesus was betrayed.

In this moment of severe disciple it seems clear to me that the church should take note of the severity of blatant disregard of God's presence. Notice the reaction to this judgment in Acts 5:11, *"So great fear came upon all the church and upon all who heard these things."* Here is the tension of this reality. Does God do that every time a believer lies? There are no recorded examples of that ever happening again. Therefore, it is wise to consider this as an exception of God's Sovereignty. After all, if it was a regular occurrence today, I don't believe we would have very many mega churches on the planet.

WHAT ABOUT THEM?

But what about those outside the Body of Christ?

In Acts 12 Herod the King of Israel at the time (his Roman name was Marcus Julius Agrippa) was giving a public speech to his people. In a moment of oratory glory, the people began to call him a god. Here is what happened:

Acts 12:21-23:

So on a set day Herod, arrayed in royal apparel, sat on his throne and gave an oration to them. And the people kept shouting, "The voice of a god and not of a man!" Then immediately an angel of the Lord struck him, because he did not give glory to God. And he was eaten by worms and died.

There is another moment of tension occurring with regard to the New Testament's clear mandate of "God reconciling the world to Himself by not counting their transgressions against them." (2Cor 5:19) Yet, here is a very clear act of swift judgment on Herod for his blasphemy. Which is it? I would propose both. I could most likely create some convincing arguments why God acted so harshly and decisively, yet I am once again satisfied with the preponderance of the weight of the New Testament pointing to God withholding judgment of unbelievers until the appointed "day."

I so appreciate what Bill Johnson says,

> An intellectual gospel is always in danger of creating a God that looks a lot like us—one that is our size. The quest for answers sometimes leads to a rejection of mystery. As a result, mystery is often treated as something intolerable, instead of a real treasure. Living with mystery is the privilege of our walk with Christ. Its importance cannot be overrated. If I understand all that is going on in my Christian life, I have an inferior Christian life. The walk of faith is to live according to the revelation we have received, in the midst of the mysteries we can't explain. That's why Christianity is called "the faith."

I'm confident I could write a whole chapter on the many illustrious malevolent despots who have ruled through the centuries and who lived treacherously, yet died seemingly without retribution from God or man. Yet once again, the weight of the New Testament carries the message of grace with such gravity that such a chapter would prove redundant.

Chapter 8 | CAN YOU LOVE THEM?

WHERE TO FROM HERE?

Some time ago, I was on the Internet researching information for this book. After going through multiple sites I stumbled on to a video link about a holiday celebration in San Francisco. It was an actual video taken on the city streets. In an instant, it became so appalling that I Xed out of the screen. I was so intensely disgusted by what I saw that for a moment it unraveled me. And instantly in my spirit I heard The Holy Spirit say, "How do you think I feel?" I remained silent. Knowing that He knows my thoughts I simply remained silent. The next question was, "Do you think that I love these people?" I was thinking... "Why do you even bother asking me these questions when you know my answer? Yes...You do love them." And the next question was, "David my son...can you love them?" You see it's real easy for me to love certain people. I intentionally spend time building relationships with all sorts of people from different cultures. However in that "see through" moment of my life I realized there are certain groups of people I find so revolting that I avoid any contact with them, at least subconsciously.

I am learning that God's love, or maybe I should say the power of His love, is supposed to leave us in a state of shock and awe. As much as I did not want to answer the question: "Do you think that I love these people..." I knew where He was taking me. Do you know that God's love is so outrageous that it shocks me? Have you ever been shocked by God's love? Why aren't more Christians shocked by His love? I'll tell you why. Because we have our little compartments of grace that work well with us but then there's this crowd over there with the piercings, tattoos and who knows what else! I could gather groups of Christians and ask them the question about "the state of the USA." Most likely, someone would eventually refer to a notable quote I used to endorse, "If God doesn't judge the US for all of its wickedness then He owes an apology to Sodom and Gomorrah." It completely contradicts the revelation of the Father that Jesus gave us.

Given the responsibilities the church has today, the role of intercession is as important as any other function. It doesn't take acute discernment of spirits to go to certain cities and places to know that you are surrounded by evil and that the city or place is entrenched in wickedness.

Some believers have come to certain cities and released severe words of judgment over that land and the people there. The challenge for me is to remember why Jesus came in these instances. Did He not give us a message of hope?

There is a difference between what is "true" and what is "truth." Yes it's true that certain cities are steeped in serious sin issues. However, the truth is they don't have to remain that way. I believe the challenge for God's people is to press in and ask the Father what He would like us to release over a particular city or people. Whenever the Kingdom of God invades, it displaces the kingdom of darkness. I call it displacement theology. Overthrow and upend, not destroy and delete.[16]

The purpose of this book is to question our use of 2 Chronicles 7:14 as the focal point of intercession in the church today. However, to complete this journey it became apparent that I had to challenge our understanding of God in general. That can and does provoke strong responses from those who have a different theology than me.

Having said that, we have already discussed the entire premise of 2 Chronicles 7:14 and the judgment of God being visited upon His people as a large contingency, versus individual discipline. In addition, we have addressed that same venue of judgment upon the world at large. In both cases I believe it is erroneous to proclaim God's character as that of a Divine Potentate who looks to release judgment and vengeance upon a disobedient church or an unredeemed world. The former would be like a father who disciplines his entire family for the bad behavior of one child. No righteous parent would institute such unfair practices. The latter would negate the entirety of Jesus' life and work as well as His Great Commission.

I urge you to reconsider the popular view that God can and/ or will at any point in our time continuum send catastrophes as judgments in response to the sinful practices of the world at large or the church He has built.

I'm always personally challenged by the friends of Job who spent a lot of time explaining to him why he was experiencing such perceived judgment in his personal life. Job 42:7-9 says,

> *After the Lord had finished speaking to Job, he said to Eliphaz the Temanite: 'I am angry with you and your two friends, for you have not spoken accurately about me, as my servant Job has. So take seven bulls and seven rams and go to my servant Job and offer a burnt offering for yourselves. My servant Job will pray for you, and I will accept his prayer on your behalf. I will not treat you as you deserve, for you have not spoken accurately about me, as my servant Job has.' So Eliphaz the Temanite, Bildad the Shuhite, and Zophar the Naamathite did as the Lord commanded them, and the Lord accepted Job's prayer. (NLT)*

There aren't enough years in my life to fully comprehend the nature of God in all of its fullness; that will take all of eternity to unfold. But I can possess some foundational aspects of God's nature now and build on that with my children's children. God is good...always. God is love...always not in between bad days or fits of rage. And God is for you...always. The Lord says, "*I know the thoughts that I think toward you, says the LORD, thoughts of peace and not of evil, to give you a future and a hope*" (Jeremiah 29:11). It is not negotiable.

My hope is that unlike Job's friends, God's people will align with the revelation that Jesus brought to us of His Dad...my Dad...our Father. There is none like Him.

Notes

[1] Term borrowed from John Wesley

[2] There are numerous exceptions to this idea throughout the OT. King David being one whereby God granted in mercy. Paul explaining in Romans 3:25-26 that is was a foretaste of what was to come in the likes of Jesus Christ. In the OT it becomes a foretaste of things to come. In the NT it becomes the center piece of the gospel.

[3] http://www.jesus-is-savior.com/Wolves/assemblies_of_god.htm

[4] David Jeremiah

[5] Strong's Number 4561

[6] Romans 7:5: *For when we were in the flesh, the sinful passions which were aroused by the law were at work in our members to bear fruit to death.* Romans 8:24-25: *O, wretched man that I am! Who will deliver me from this body of death? I thank God—through Jesus Christ our Lord!* Galatians 5:22-24: *But the fruit of the Spirit is love, joy, peace, longsuffering, kindness, goodness, faithfulness, gentleness, self-control. Against such there is no law. And those who are Christ's have crucified the flesh with its passions and desires.*

[7] However Paul makes it clear that the Cross is only the starting point in our journey with The Lord. 2 Corinthians 3:18: *But we all, with unveiled face, beholding as in a mirror the glory of the Lord, are being transformed into the same image from glory to glory, just as by the Spirit of the Lord.*

[8] http://www.simplemarriage.net/the-virtuous-marriage-justice.html

[9] Unfortunately some have taken this clear truth quoted in 2 Peter 3:9, *The Lord is not slack concerning His promise, as some count slackness, but is longsuffering toward us not willing that any should perish but that all should come to repentance,* and carried it to the heretical claims of Universalism.

[10] Dr. Martin Luther King

[11]John Wesley

[12]Source unknown

[13]The context is most certainly the captivity of Israel for their continued disobedience of God's Law. On the other hand the principle is most certainly corroborated by Paul in 1 Timothy 2:1-4: *Therefore I exhort first of all that supplications, prayers, intercessions, and giving of thanks be made for all men, for kings and all who are in authority, that we may lead a quiet and peaceable life in all godliness and reverence. For this is good and acceptable in the sight of God our Savior, who desires all men to be saved and to come to the knowledge of the truth.*

[14]Sojourner Truth (1797-1883): *Ain't I A Woman?* Delivered 1851-Women's Convention, Akron, Ohio

[15]*Kittles Theological Dictionary of The New Testament* ,Volume 1 Pages 407-445.

[16]The book of Jonah clearly portrays this as God's heart. Jonah demanded judgment upon a people he despised. God on the other hand wanted mercy to triumph over judgment. 4:10-11: *Then the LORD said, "You feel sorry about the plant, though you did nothing to put it there. It came quickly and died quickly. But Nineveh has more than 120,000 people living in spiritual darkness, not to mention all the animals. Shouldn't I feel sorry for such a great city?* (NLT)

About the Author

David Addesa is the senior pastor of Harvest Assembly of God, Chesapeake, Virginia. He received his Masters in Biblical Studies from Regent University. David is passionate about revival and seeing transformation in the lives of individuals, families, and regions. Together, he and his wife Lisa, have thee amazing children, Hannah, Emma, and Noah.

23591266R00066